Axed
between
the
Ears

I'd like to dedicate this book to the pupils
and English teachers I have worked with
and without whom there would be no book.
In particular I would like to thank John Wilkins,
Roger Palmer and Margaret James.
Next to the bloke who mends my burst pipes,
I like them best.

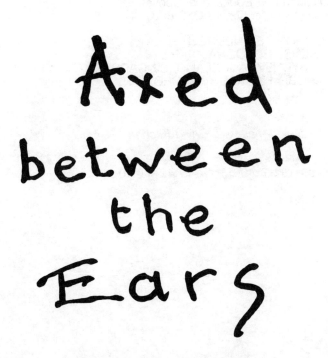

Axed between the Ears

A Poetry Anthology

Edited by
David Kitchen

HEINEMANN
EDUCATIONAL

Heinemann Educational
a division of Heinemann Educational Books Ltd
Halley Court, Jordan Hill, Oxford OX2 8EJ

OXFORD LONDON EDINBURGH
MADRID ATHENS BOLOGNA PARIS
MELBOURNE SYDNEY AUCKLAND SINGAPORE TOKYO
IBADAN NAIROBI HARARE GABORONE
PORTSMOUTH NH (USA)

First published 1987
    93 94 95 96 18 17 16 15 14 13 12 11 10

ISBN 0 435 14530 4

Cover design by Caroline Allison

Typeset by Ampersand Typesetting Ltd, Bournemouth, Dorset
Printed in England by Clays Ltd, St Ives plc

CONTENTS

Acknowledgements

The editor and publishers wish to thank the following for permission to reproduce copyright material. It has not been possible to contact all copyright holders, and the publishers would be glad to hear from any unacknowledged sources.

Stainer & Bell Ltd for 'Run the Film Backwards' by Sydney Carter; Macdonald Publishers for 'The Playground' by Michael Rosen from *Wheel Around The World*; Roger McGough and Jonathan Cape Ltd for 'The Lesson', 'Nooligan' and 'Streemin' from *In the Classroom*; Idris Jones for 'First Day'; Corgi Books for 'Petronella' from *It's World That Makes Love Go Round*, ed. Ken Geering, © 1966 by Jeffrey Grenfell-Hill; Gerald Duckworth & Co. Ltd for 'The Choice' by Dorothy Parker from *The Collected Dorothy Parker*; Hodder & Stoughton Limited for 'Daily London Recipe', 'Declaration of Intent' and 'The Appeal' by Steve Turner from *Up to Date*; Stewart Henderson for 'Mabel' and 'A Danish Pastry Lament'; Philomena Broderick for 'Friday Nights'; Elizabeth Jennings and Macmillan for 'Friends' from *My Secret Brother*; André Deutsch Ltd for 'What's the Matter?' by Michael Rosen from *When Did You Last Wash Your Feet?*; Charles Causley and Macmillan for 'Green Man in the Garden' from *Collected Poems*; Mike Johnson for 'Save It for the Kids'; Adrian Mitchell and Jonathan Cape Ltd for 'Old Age Report' from *Ride the Nightmare*, and 'Dumb Insolence' from *The Ape Man Cometh*; Debi Hinton for 'A Sequence of Poems for my Daughter'; Mary Dorcey for 'First Love'; Roger Palmer for 'Love Grows Old Too'; The Estate of Mrs Frieda Lawrence Ravagh and Laurence Pollinger Ltd for 'Beautiful Old Age' by D. H. Lawrence; Anvil Press for 'In Oak Terrace' by Tony Connor from *New and Selected Poems* (1982); Enitharmon Press for 'Geriatric Ward' by Phoebe Hesketh; Margot Stewart for 'Brain Damaged'; Herbert Williams for 'The Inheritor'; Poetry Wales Press for 'Pneumoconiosis' by Duncan Bush from *Aquarium*; MBA Literary Agents for 'The Song of the Wagondriver' by B. S. Johnson; Sally Flood for 'A Working Mum'; John Murray (Publishers) Ltd for 'Meditation on the A30' by John Betjeman from *Collected Poems*; Harry Graham and Edward Arnold (Publishers) Ltd for 'Quiet Fun' from *Ruthless Rhymes*; Bryn Griffiths for 'Ianto the Undertaker'; W. Bridges-Adam for 'Notting Hill Polka'; Pat Arrowsmith for 'Freedom'; Vernon Scannell for 'Peerless Jim Driscoll'; Michael Rosen for 'Parents' Sayings'; Dorothy Byrne for 'Nice Men'; Leslie Norris for 'A Girl's Song'; Gomer Press for 'Our Budgie' by Harri Webb from *The Green Desert*; Harper & Row Publishers Inc. for 'Travelling through the Dark' from *Stories That Could Be True* by William Stafford © 1977; Anthony Thwaite and Secker & Warburg for 'Hedgehog' from *Poems 1953–1983* (Secker & Warburg, 1984); Anthony Thompson for 'Death of a Cat'; Vernon Scannell for 'A Case of Murder' and 'Peerless Jim Driscoll'; Michael Joseph Ltd for 'The Dog Lovers' by Spike Milligan from *Small Dreams of a Scorpion*; Irene McLeod for 'Lone Dog'; David Gill for 'Killing a Whale'; Roy Fuller for 'The National Union of Children'; George Sassoon for 'Atrocities' by Siegfried Sassoon; James Simmons for 'Kill the Children'; Roger McGough and Jonathan Cape Ltd for 'Identification' from *GIG*; Oxford University Press for 'First Blood' from *Out-of Bounds* by Jon Stallworthy (1963); Peter Roche for 'Plug In, Turn On, Look Out'; Adrian Mitchell for 'Requirements in the Shelter'; Maureen Burge for 'The Diet'; Pam Ayres for 'Eat, Drink and Be Sick'; Geraint Jarman for 'The Hayes, Cardiff'; Gomer Press for 'Never Again' by Harri Webb from *A Crown for Branwen*; Adrian Henri for 'Adrian Henri's Talking After Christmas Blues' © 1967; Oxford University Press for 'A Martian Sends a Postcard Home' from *A Martian Sends a Postcard Home* by Craig Raine (1979); Landesman Publishers, 8 Duncan Terrace, London, for 'After We've Gone' by Fran Landesman from *The Ballad of the Sad Young Men and Other Verse*; Edwin Brock for 'Song of the Battery Hen'.

All photographs are copyright and are reproduced by courtesy of the following:
Popperfoto pp. 9, 34 and 87; Network pp. 19, 26, 28 and 88; Chris Fairclough p. 26; Topham p. 31; Betty Rawlings p. 56; Barnaby's Picture Library p. 58; RSPCA p. 57; Greenpeace p. 70; Keystone p. 78.

Illustrations by Dave Farris pp. 40, 54, 64-5, 96-7; Murray Aikman pp. 2, 5, 8, 21, 68, 69, 93, 95; Alan Burton pp. 10, 50-1, 89; Colin Robinson pp. 12-13, 44-5, 46-7, 76, 77, 82-3, 85, 99.

Introduction

It's easy enough to stick together a selection of poems that will please the teachers reading them. Putting together a selection which will please teachers and pupils is an altogether more troublesome task. The fact is that they don't always have the same tastes.

My reaction to the problem has been to be biased. It's the pupils who have to read the poems, have to discuss them, have to write about them. So it's the pupils who deserve the first say.

I do not claim that this is a radically new idea or a radically new kind of anthology. I do claim, however, that when reading this book Kingy and Bazzer described some of the poems as 'dead brill'. Even more remarkably, Andrew Ella, king of the report card and the flying pair of compasses, said that a few of the poems were 'quite good'. This is the first time in living memory that Andrew has described something within the four walls of a school as anything other than 'rubbish'.

As the anthology is intended for those in their later years at secondary school, some of the suggestions for work have an eye directly fixed on the final examination. Hence, certain poems offer the option of a fairly straightforward piece of comprehension work. Many others give the opportunity to use the poem, sometimes with related material, as a stimulus for creative writing.

I hope this doesn't obscure the fact that at the heart of this book is a collection of poems that have evoked strong positive response from pupils. Perhaps the best way to introduce the poems themselves is to allow a group the chance to dip into the book and make one or two choices of their own. When we were working on the poems for the anthology, we found that most classes actually wanted to read out some of the poems aloud to their friends. When this happens, you have broken down the first barrier of prejudice against poetry.

Let's face it: most poems have about as much effect in a classroom as a feather dropping from a great height on an elephant's back. I hope that some of these fall more like an axe between the ears.

David Kitchen

Notes

While all the poems can be read privately, a few were chosen, not because of the response they received when read quietly, but because they worked when properly introduced and performed. The five poems that fall into this category are 'Pneumoconiosis', 'Daily London Recipe', 'Ianto the Undertaker', 'First Blood' and 'A Martian Sends a Postcard Home'.

These are not the only poems which benefit greatly from good performance. Others which we have found to benefit particularly from a teacher's streak of the dramatic include 'The Farmer's Wife', 'Gresford Disaster', 'The Ruined Maid', 'Green Beret' and 'The Identification'.

The suggestions for written or oral work have been included because every teacher has a limited supply of time and hence of time to create new ideas. An effort has been made to include a good deal of variety, not only in the types of work but in the amount of direction given. In addition, the quantity of material available ought to give plenty of scope for personal selection. If teachers were to diligently follow up every suggestion for written work in this book, some of the pupils would be grandparents before the course was over.

The choice of which poems have attendant work and which are left to stand on their own is, to some extent, arbitrary. Certain poems seemed to cry out for a particular approach and with others it appeared best to let them stand without comment. As far as has been feasible, I have been led by the twin aims of responding to my own pupils' reactions and my own pupils' needs (aims which on occasion come into conflict, of course).

As far as possible, all that needs to be said has been included alongside the poems themselves. However, that still leaves a few additional comments about certain individual poems and sequences.

Riddles

The answers to these are a saw, coffins, a motorcycle and an onion.

Friends

Apart from capturing with sparkling clarity a feeling that nearly everyone shares, Elizabeth Jennings's poem provides a helpful introduction to rhyme and rhythm. The rhyme scheme is regular – a b c b d e f e – with a similar pattern in the second verse. The metrical pattern is of an iambic tetrameter followed by an iambic trimeter. (The one exception is the third line which is half a foot short.) The stresses are also fairly regular and the most obvious exception, at the start of the second stanza, serves to emphasise the theme of the poem.

The Farmer's Wife

Before using this poem, you may want to refer to related material on werewolves in order to inform what is often a lively discussion.

Green Man in the Garden

If you choose to take up the idea of the creature of the night suggested in the text, one approach is to develop an urban equivalent of the green man. Perhaps he might be grey and speak with an asthmatic smoker's wheeze. His haunts might include rubbish tips and derelict buildings, his jacket might be made of corrugated iron . . .

Sequence of poems on old age

For further information about the situations that elderly people face, a useful contact is Age Concern, 60 Pitcairn Road, Mitcham, Surrey CR43 3LL.

The Inheritor

The poem has a happy personal postscript in that the author's son came successfully through the operation.

Travelling through the Dark

The poem provides an opportunity to discuss the situation with which the writer is faced. It is not so much a moral dilemma as the problem of doing the right thing even when the task is distasteful. An obvious parallel is taking a loved pet who is old and sick to the vet to be put down.

   The opportunity for anecdotal reminiscence can be developed in conjunction with the next poem, 'Death of a Cat'.

A Case of Murder

The master of the story in which guilt and horror grip the main character is Edgar Allan Poe. This poem echoes his tale of 'The Black Cat'. As Poe's style is very much of his age, a little judicious editing and simplifying can make the use of his story that much more effective.

Sequence of poems on conflict

There is a mountain of material available on the theme of conflict. However, one play deals particularly with the gap between the boast and the reality just as 'Nooligan' and 'Atrocities' do. The play in question is The Long, the Short and the Tall by Willis Hall (published by Heinemann).

   Ho Thien's poem 'Green Beret' looks at the Vietnamese conflict from North Vietnam's point of view. As a number of history syllabuses now deal with the war in Vietnam, it is worth a moment or two of liaison to see what documentary material is available within school or even to synchronise the use of this particular poem with the appropriate moment in the history course. As the poem is written from a committed standpoint, it presents an opportunity to discuss what details reveal that commitment/bias. It also offers the chance to work in pairs with one pupil telling about the incident from the soldier's angle and the other from the boy's viewpoint.

   The chance to write from a variety of standpoints is developed further in the work suggested alongside 'Kill the Children' and 'The Identification'.

First Blood

This poem, in particular, repays a thoughtful introduction by the teacher. Obviously the poem is a very honest, straightforward account of an involvement of an act of unthinking cruelty with a strong sense of guilt and remorse following the deed.

   The written questions that accompany the poem by no means exhaust the areas that can be discussed. There is, for example, the effect of the short sentences. Again, there is the difference between the practice with paper targets and the shooting of a living creature; the poem, indeed, pivots on the realisation that the target has a life of its own.

Whether the questions are attempted orally or on paper they fall into two sections: **a–d** are mainly factual while **e–h** concentrate more on the question of response to the killing.

Adrian Henri's Talking After Christmas Blues

It might seem a little Scrooge-like to dwell on Christmas celebrations that go wrong or never happen. However, the truth seems to be that the cheery, traditional, family Christmas is the exception rather than the rule.

Visual reinforcement of some of the situations which might make it difficult to enjoy Christmas can be very helpful in assisting those who are not choosing to write from direct personal experience. A 'Don't Drink and Drive' poster, a picture of a solitary old person, photographs of dossers, old and young, can all help to form the seed of a story.

It may sound gloomy described like this but it need not be if it leads to a certain amount of reflection on what can be done to help. For example, hospitals ought to be utterly cheerless places on 25 December but people's kindness and goodwill often transform them.

So much for the details. At the end of the day, what will matter is whether anything that has been read has made an impact.

Run the Film Backwards

When I was eighty-seven
they took me from my coffin;
they found a flannel nightshirt
for me to travel off in.

All innocent and toothless
I used to lie in bed,
still trailing clouds of glory
from the time when I was dead.

The cruel age of sixty-five
put paid to my enjoyment;
I had to wear a bowler hat
and go to my employment.

But at the age of sixty
I found I had a wife.
And that explains the children.
(I'd wondered all my life.)

I kept on growing younger
and randier and stronger
till at the age of twenty-one
I had a wife no longer.

With mini-skirted milkmaids
I frolicked in the clover;
the cuckoo kept on calling me
until my teens were over.

Then algebra and cricket
and sausages a-cooking,
and puffing at a cigarette
when teacher wasn't looking.

The trees are getting taller,
the streets are getting wider.
My mother is the world to me;
and soon I'll be inside her.

And now, it is so early,
there's nothing I can see.
Before the world, or after?
Wherever can I

be?

SYDNEY CARTER

If you could run the film of your own life backwards, what incidents would you remember?

Your first cigarette?
Starting a part-time job?
A nightmare?
Breaking an ankle?
Your sister's wedding?
Getting into a pub?
A divorce in the family?

A particular holiday?
The birth of a younger brother?
A brush with the police?
Breaking something valuable?
Starting a new school?
Getting caught pinching apples?

'When I was ...'

Choose one incident and try to bring that moment in the past to life again.

Don't just say what happened. Try to create the atmosphere of the moment. What details can you remember? How did you feel at the time? How did other people react?

If you find enough to say, you might write about just one incident but, if you have time, write about two or three other incidents in the same way.

The Choice

He'd have given me rolling lands,
Houses of marble, and billowing farms,
Pearls, to trickle between my hands,
Smouldering rubies, to circle my arms.
You . . . you'd only a lilting song,
Only a melody, happy and high,
You were sudden and swift and strong . . .
Never a thought for another had I.

He'd have given me laces rare,
Dresses that glimmered with frosty sheen,
Shining ribbons to wrap my hair,
Horses to draw me, as fine as a queen.
You . . . you'd only to whistle low,
Gaily I followed wherever you led.
I took you, and I let him go . . .
Somebody ought to examine my head!

DOROTHY PARKER

The Playground

In the playground
At the back of our house
There have been some changes.

They said the climbing frame was
NOT SAFE
So they sawed it down.

They said the paddling pool was
NOT SAFE
So they drained it dry.

They said the see-saw was
NOT SAFE
So they took it away.

They said the sandpit was
NOT SAFE
So they fenced it in.

They said the playground was
NOT SAFE
So they locked it up.

Sawn down
Drained dry
Taken away
Fenced in
Locked up

How do you feel?
Safe?

MICHAEL ROSEN

'Not Wanted'

They picked the sides
For the game
And she was left over
NOT WANTED

They said you can choose any subjects
So long as the teachers agree
To your suitability
And they didn't
NOT WANTED

They wanted people with experience
He didn't have any
Because they had always required
People with experience
NOT WANTED

**See if you can write your own piece
called 'Not Wanted'.**

3

Peerless Jim Driscoll

I saw Jim Driscoll fight in nineteen ten.
That takes you back a bit. You don't see men
Like Driscoll any more. The breed's died out.
There's no one fit to lace his boots about.
All right son. Have your laugh. You know it all.
You think these mugs today that cuff and maul
Their way through ten or fifteen threes can fight:
They hardly know their left hand from their right.
But Jim, he knew: he never slapped or swung,
His left had flickered like a cobra's tongue
And when he followed with the old one-two
Black lightning of those fists would dazzle you.
By Jesus he could hit. I've never seen
A sweeter puncher: every blow as clean
As silver. *Peerless Jim* the papers named him,
And yet he never swaggered, never bragged.
I saw him once when he got properly tagged –
A sucker punch from nowhere on the chin –
And he was hurt; but all he did was grin
And nod as if to say, 'I asked for that.'

No one was ever more worth looking at;
Up there beneath the ache of arc-lamps he
Was just like what we'd love our sons to be
Or like those gods you've heard about at school . . .
Well, yes, I'm old; and maybe I'm a fool.
I only saw him once outside the ring
And I admit I found it disappointing.
He looked just – I don't know – just ordinary,
And smaller, too, than what I thought he'd be:
An ordinary man in fact, like you or me.

VERNON SCANNELL

a   Who is speaking in this poem and to whom?

b   What do you think is meant by 'there's no one fit to lace his boots about'?

c   How are today's boxers described in the poem?

d   What does the poem tell you about Jim Driscoll's personality?

e   Why did the speaker in the poem admire Driscoll even when the boxer got
     caught by an amateurish punch?

f   Explain how the last few lines contrast with the rest of the poem.

g   What evidence can you find in the words used that the speaker might have been
     exaggerating Jim's ability?

4

Streemin

Im in the botom streme
Which meens Im not brigth
dont like reading
cant hardly write

but all these divishns
arnt reely fair
look at the cemtery
no streemin there

ROGER McGOUGH

First Day

I am teaching again.

Sitting on the edge of the table
I turn on the old tricks
Like a performing animal.

They call me Sir,
Go out and fetch me chalk,
And I hardly recognise myself.

Lunch-time, the talk in the staff-room
I recognise from past years,
Old attitudes, jokes, introductions.
Then I wander out into the sunlight
Where the boys play ball
And the sun glares off the tarmac.

A teacher beside me talks.
He has just applied for a job at ICI
After 30 years teaching.

He doesn't like this school either.

Please God do not leave chalk in my pockets too long.

J. I. JONES

The Lesson

A poem that raises the question:
Should there be capital punishment in schools?

Chaos ruled OK in the classroom
as bravely the teacher walked in
the nooligans ignored him
his voice was lost in the din

'The theme for today is violence
and homework will be set
I'm going to teach you a lesson
one that you'll never forget'

He picked on a boy who was shouting
and throttled him then and there
then garotted the girl behind him
(the one with grotty hair)

Then sword in hand he hacked his way
between the chattering rows
'First come, first severed' he declared
'fingers, feet, or toes'

He threw the sword at a latecomer
it struck with deadly aim
then pulling out a shotgun
he continued with his game

The first blast cleared the backrow
(where those who skive hang out)
they collapsed like rubber dinghies
when the plug's pulled out

'Please may I leave the room sir?'
a trembling vandal enquired
'Of course you may' said the teacher
put the gun to his temple and fired

The Head popped a head round the doorway
to see why a din was being made
nodded understandingly
then tossed in a grenade

And when the ammo was well spent
with blood on every chair
Silence shuffled forward
with its hands up in the air

The teacher surveyed the carnage
the dying and the dead
He waggled a finger severely
'Now let that be a lesson' he said

ROGER McGOUGH

September

4 Monday

First day back and I get 5G as a form. Who did I upset last year? I cannot believe the state of Karen Clees' hair. How does she make it go luminous pink anyway? She scowled when I asked her.

Darren Culthorpe actually attended today. The rest of the class say that's it for the term.

5 Tuesday

Thank goodness. I get a double period with my first form today. They actually look as though they want to learn. When I enter the classroom they jump to their feet and wait silently. A change from 5G; you're lucky if anyone notices when you come in. And when they do, all you get is, "Oh, it's you".

Darren was absent.

6 Wednesday

Darren was missing for morning and afternoon registration but managed to be well enough to come in and eat his lunch in the canteen. This is apparently a regular feature of his behaviour. The class say that he's into "food studies" but not much else. My fourth form butchered "Macbeth" this afternoon. They said it was "dead boring". I'm not surprised the way they read.

Of course, if a teacher were to write about you and your friends, it would all be complimentary . . . wouldn't it?

Try to put yourself inside the head of a teacher for a short while and imagine what he or she might write in his or her diary.

How would your group compare with a first form class?
Which individuals might get a mention?
What would really depress a teacher?
What might brighten up the day?

Don't say which teacher is supposed to be writing the diary. Let your readers use their imagination on that.

Declaration of Intent

She said she'd
love me for eternity
but managed to reduce
it to eight months
for good behaviour.
She said we fitted
like a hand in a glove
but then the hot
weather came and such
accessories weren't needed.
She said the future
was ours but the deeds
were made out in
her name.
She said I was
the only one who
understood completely

and then she left me
and said she knew
that I'd understand completely.

STEVE TURNER

Mabel

When I was a lad of tender years
I took upon myself
To find a love to fill my life
Upon her lay my wealth.

How I remember Mabel
She was to be my mate
She played left back for Chelsea
And drank Guinness by the crate.

She used to smell so sweetly —
Yardley's after shave,
For a hobby she beat up navvies
My dear sweet Mabel the brave.

She had tattoos all over her body —
On her right hand 'I love you',
And on her back in full graphic colour
The battle of Waterloo.

But alas the day arrived
Mabel and I became aloof,
She was caught by twenty policemen
Stripping lead off the parish church roof.

They've taken away my Mabel
But I still have one of her gloves,
On it lingers the smell of Guinness
Come back Mabel, sweet Mabel, my love.

STEWART HENDERSON

Friday Nights

Noreen goes there every Friday with Brenda.
She hopes Barry will send her a message over from the other side
(and eventually be his bride),
She is wearing her best pink dress
and her green patent leather shoes.
She looks a mess.
So does Brenda.
Big friend of hers.
Boys laugh as she passes,
laugh as the strobe bounces off her glasses.
Brenda's bottom has been pinched by Barry's mate.
Is this some sort of sign?
Will Barry aquiesce?
She can only guess.
God, the torture of these Friday Nights, this hateful place.
Still she must endure it, she must.
In the power of love she must place her trust.

PHILOMENA BRODERICK

What sort of place do Noreen and Brenda go to on Friday nights?

Why do they go?

What do we find out about their appearance?

What evidence is there about whether or not they enjoy Friday nights?

Try to write your own piece called 'Friday Night'.

- At what sort of place might you and your friends gather on Friday night?

- What is the conversation like?
- What happens there?
- What parts of the evening are enjoyable?

- What do you do if it gets boring?
- How do you get on with the others?
- How do they behave?

Friends

I fear it's very wrong of me
And yet I must admit,
When someone offers friendship
I want the *whole* of it.
I don't want everybody else
To share my friends with me.
At least, I want *one* special one,
Who, indisputably.

Likes me much more than all the rest,
Who's always on my side,
Who never cares what others say,
Who lets me come and hide
Within his shadow, in his house —
It doesn't matter where —
Who lets me simply be myself,
Who's always, *always* there.

ELIZABETH JENNINGS

The Farmer's Wife

'Spring is the time for a wedding
And I'll be married in May
When the thorn is white and from first light
My young lambs frolic and play,'
Said Jack, the farmer of Fairness
Watching the mountain side
And the high house where by her glittering hair
He could see Julie Ann, his bride.

His mother said, 'Julie Ann
Is not the woman for you,
When she comes down here, the horses rear
And the farm dogs whimper and growl.'
Said Jack, 'I will marry my Julie
So hold your tongue, screech owl.'

White and gold was Julie
When she stood by the side of Jack
And the old man made them man and wife
In the High God's painted house.
Only a mother noticed
The slim girl's eyes like a knife
Touch a little brown dog who turned and fled
As if it fled for its life,
Fled to the farm in the valley
Where Jack made a feast for his wife.

White light on the bedroom window
And a farmer jerks out of sleep
Hearing far below in a faint meadow
The brawl of his murdered sheep.
His wife does not lie beside him
And he thinks, 'While I slumbered she went,
To save from the wolf – she is half myself –
The sheep that I love, our sheep.'
He did not notice the puppy
Slashed from groin to jaw
Still, lying in its own red blood,
As he stumbled out of the door.

But notice he did the nightgown
Of his wife by the river bed
And how two small feet with four claws meet,
And the hair prickled up on his head;
For the ravaged sheep lay savaged
Under the light of the moon
And a she-wolf skulked in the brushwood
With a glittering golden ring.

O he has no silver bullet
And what are bullets of lead
To the were-wolf there whose red eyes stare
Under the light of the moon?
His mother hears a gun shot
In her house alone on the moor
And waits for the bride of a son who died
And a scraping on the door.

ANON.

a   What is it that wakes Jack from sleep?

b   What does he fail to notice as he leaves the house?

c   What has happened to his wife?

d   What evidence is there to show what has happened?

e   Why does Jack need a silver bullet?

f   There is a gun shot – what do you think has happened?

Green Man in the Garden

Green man in the garden
  Staring from the tree,
Why do you look so long and hard
  Through the pane at me?

Your eyes are dark as holly,
  Of sycamore your horns,
Your bones are made of elder-branch,
  Your teeth are made of thorns.

Your hat is made of ivy-leaf,
  Of bark your dancing shoes,
And evergreen and green and green
  Your jacket and shirt and trews.

Leave your house and leave your land
  And throw away the key,
And never look behind, he creaked,
  And come and live with me.

I bolted up the window,
  I bolted up the door,
I drew the blind that I should find
  The green man never more.

But when I softly turned the stair
  As I went up to bed,
I saw the green man standing there.
  Sleep well, my friend, he said.

CHARLES CAUSLEY

A Creature of the Night

There is a scratching on the window pane.

You ignore it.

It continues.

You snuggle under the covers.

The scratching doesn't go away.

You look out nervously from under the covers and realise that you haven't drawn the curtains properly.

There is an eye – or is it eyes? – looking at you.

To your horror, you find yourself getting out of bed and heading for the window. It's as if your normal self has lost control of your body.

Reaching the window, you draw back the curtains to reveal the creature and you find your hand reaching to open the latch on the window . . .

'Petronella'

'Petronella darling don't play down there,
Come and have tea with Auntie and me,
It's nice and sunny here on the lawn
And there's lots of strawberry jam.
We'll even let you pick the currants
And leave the rest of the scone.
Petra, please, don't kick the cat,
And do stop picking your nose.

Yes, she's seven this year
And so affectionate too.
Don't throw stones at Mummy dear,
They might go in her eyes.
Auntie has brought you a present
My love, come, kiss her and say
Hullo – Petra! No, I think the little
Dear said 'Oh! well.'

Petra don't dig up the dahlias
And do give your knickers a tug.
I don't like you playing down there
My love, the goblins will catch
You I'm sure – you'll kill them!
Well, come and have tea with Auntie and me,
And we'll let you drink out of the saucer,
It's one of her off days you know.

Petronella! You've now gone too far,
You've covered the table with sod,
I know you don't care, but Auntie
Is here, and she loves little girls like you.
Leave the dahlias alone,
No, we don't want a hole,
And do stop screaming down there –
Oh! dear, she's found Uncle George . . .'

JEFFREY GRENFELL-HILL

Save It for the Kids

It's all right, I understand,
I won't blame, beg or demand,
I just came to shake your hand
And tell you thanks a lot.

Never asking why, no doubt
That's what love is all about:
Falling in, then falling out
Never knowing what.

Didn't we love openly,
Clean and without secrecy?
Best to leave it honestly
Parting like old friends.

Explanations are no use
From discretion's point of view.
Love begins with no excuse:
That's how it should end.

Every ship is bound to sail
Daylight doesn't die, it pales,
When they ask you how we failed
Say we never did.

If you love him more than me
That's the way it ought to be,
Don't waste your apologies
Save them for the kids.

Something old, something new,
Something borrowed, something blue,
Something finished, something through,
Something finalised.

Something promised warm and wide,
Gushing groom and blushing bride,
Someone who came by and tried
Not to act surprised.

So to bachelor buffs again,
Conquests and rebuffs again,
Shirts with unpressed cuffs again,
Blind dates and tasteless ties.

And if tomorrow we should meet
And the kids ask who is he,
Tell them it's just somebody
We seem to recognise.

MICK JOHNSON

Why do you think the poem is called 'Save It for the Kids'?

How does the writer want the break-up to be?

What is the tone of the poem?

It's always sad when a relationship of any sort breaks up. **See if you can write a letter in which you tell a close friend about the break-up of a relationship.**

It could be but needn't necessarily be a relationship in which you were involved. It could simply be something you've observed.

If you're basing it on real life, you might choose to change the names of the characters.

The hard part is to capture the reactions and the feelings of the different people involved.

74 March Street
Cathays
Cardiff

18 February

Dear Sue

What a strange couple of months I've had. No one could have enjoyed Christmas more than I did. Since then everything seems to have turned sour...

A Sequence of Poems for my Daughter, Christmas '83

I

Why are you in bed, Mama?

I'm tired,
The part of me that kept my back straight
And my hands busy with
    cooking
    cleaning
    caring
has broken.
I'm tired.

Why are you crying, Mama?

I'm unhappy.
The part of me that kept my mouth smiling
and my heart busy with
    caring,
    soothing,
    coping,
has broken.
I'm unhappy.

II

Mothers should not cry,
    or lie in bed.
My mother did not lie in bed and cry –
She had five of us, there was no time.
I, who have only one, have time enough.
I am worn out trying to be too many people –
Mother, father,
I try all roles – breadwinner, houskeeper.

My mother had a maid.
If I am too tired,
    the housework does not get done,
We have chips for dinner,
And the dishes pile up like guilt in the sink.

How can I expect you to understand?
You are twelve and
    twelve is a time for being twelve and silly.
How grey my thoughts are today.
I cannot be all that you expect of me
    any more than
You can be all I expect of you.

III

For my Christmas present next year
I would like:
    someone else to be my mother
    someone else to buy the presents
    (and worry if we can afford them)
    someone else to buy the food
    and do the cooking –
While I take a long walk in the country
    by myself.

IV

When you were young,
You took the love I gave you
And gave me all you had,
Held nothing back.
Things were easier then.

Now, twelve years from the womb
You face me:
    'This is what I am', you say,
    'This is who I am.
    You gave me life (a dubious gift –
    double-edged, welcome and unwelcome),
Now you have to live with me.'

Well, that is so,
and we are bound as inextricably to each other
as if the birthcord had never been cut,
pulling and pushing.
Why did I think it would be easy?

V

I love you –
Child of my womb
Child of my heart
Pain-bringer
Love-giver
Joy-maker
Time-taker
Heart-healer
Daughter mine.

DEBI HINTON

Poetry is a little bit like painting: without contrast there is very little to see. In one painting, the contrast may be between the character in the foreground and the background setting. In another, the contrast may be mainly in terms of the different colours used. Contrasts vary but they remain important, whatever they are.

Look carefully at 'A Sequence of Poems for my Daughter, Christmas '83'.

Where can you see contrasts?

Write them down in your own words and make sure you describe both sides of the contrast.

If you manage to do that fairly thoroughly, you will find that you have a clear description of what the sequence of poems is about.

Looking at the contrasts will not tell you everything about a poem but it will tell you a great deal. At the same time it will help you to understand a poem and to write about it.

Two other poems where contrasts can be seen at work are 'The Choice' (on page 2) and 'Poor but Honest' (on page 52).

First Love

You were tall and beautiful.
You wore your long brown hair
wound about your head,
your neck stood clear and full
as the stem of a vase.
You held my hand in yours
and we walked slowly, talking
of small familiar happenings
and of the lost secrets of
your childhood. It seems it was

Always autumn then.
The amber trees shook. We laughed
in a wind that cracked the leaves
from black boughs and set them scuffling
about our feet, for me to trample still
and kick in orange clouds
about your face. We would climb dizzy
to the cliff's edge and stare down
at a green and purple sea, the

Wind howling in our ears, as it
tore the breath from white cheeked waves.
You steadied me against
the wheeling screech of gulls, and i
loved to think that but for your strength
i would tumble to the rocks below
to the fated death, your stories made me
dream of. i don't remember
that i looked in your eyes or that we
ever asked an open question. Our thoughts

Passed through our blood, it seemed,
and the slightest pressure of our hands
decided all issues wordlessly.
We watched in silence by the shore
the cold spray against our skin,
in mutual need of the water's fierce,
inhuman company, that gave promise
of some future, timeless refuge from
all the fixed anxieties of our world.
As we made for home

We faced into the wind, my thighs
were grazed by its icy teeth, you
gathered your coat about me and i
hurried our steps towards home, fire
and the comfort of your sweet strong tea.
We moved bound in step.
You sang me songs of Ireland's sorrows
and of proud women, loved and lost.
I knew then, they set for me
a brilliant stage of characters, who

Even now, can seem more real
than my most intimate friends.
We walked together, hand in hand.
You were tall and beautiful,
you wore your long brown hair wound
about your head, your neck stood
clear and full as the stem of a vase.
I was young – you were my mother
and it seems, it was always
autumn then.

MARY DORCEY

Riddles

The joy of a riddle is trying to puzzle out what is being described.

1

I'll rip and tear my victims,
I've teeth from top to toe,
Yet place your hand upon me
And, at your will, I'll go.

2

People who make them don't want them,
People who buy them don't use them,
People who use them don't realise.

3

Against the dark night sky,
I see it turn its head
Its one eye gleams
And stares at me, unblinking.
I hear it cough,
I hear its hungry roar
And I am afraid.

4

I bite when bitten
But have no teeth,
I have no tears for you
Though you for me
Have tears but no grief.

Having puzzled over other people's riddles, it's enjoyable to be able to create your own puzzle in words.

You need to decide on a fairly ordinary object – for example, a chair.
Then you need to get a number of people to talk about that object while you write down what they say. (Young children often come up with interesting and unusual descriptions.)

For a chair, you might get a set like this:

- It's covered in flowers and sags in the middle.
- It's got legs and cushions.
- It's held together by eight nuts and bolts.
- They make good spaceships if you turn them on their side.
- I go to sleep in mine.
- The dog's ruined most of ours.

Out of these you can create your own word puzzle, getting rid of any pieces of description that give the game away and adapting it to suit your purposes.

So your final piece might read:

A good spaceship
Though covered in flowers
A good bedroom
But a bad kennel
Eight nuts, eight bolts
A nice pair of legs
And another nice pair

Some objects are easier to create puzzle descriptions of than others so you may need to experiment.

Love Grows Old Too

When you and I were younger,
We used to long for bed;
'That's all you ever think about!'
Was what you always said.

By the time we'd both reached middle age,
The time was never right.
The only time we ever touched
Was just to kiss goodnight.

When we were in our sixties
We slept in separate beds,
And the only loving we enjoyed
Came in paperbacks we read.

And now we don't have long to go,
We just turn off the light.
We drop our teeth in bedside mugs
And politely say 'Goodnight'.

ROGER PALMER

In this poem Roger Palmer has taken four moments in a couple's life to show the way that time changes what happens.

It's not only time that changes the picture. Two people may describe the same situation or person in very different ways.

How would various people describe *you*?

Choose three people – family or friends, it doesn't matter – and write down in rough what you think they would say about you.

Before you write up a fair copy, get a friend to read what you've written. Is it realistic? Can it be improved?

If you want a title for this, you might call it **The Real Me?**

Now, what about a typical evening at home: how would two different people describe it?

You might choose to write from your own point of view and from your mother's point of view.

You might look at it from the angle of a visiting friend or a sister or even a nosey neighbour with an ear against the wall ...

Old Age Report

When a man's too ill or old to work
We punish him.
Half his income is taken away
Or all of it vanishes and he gets pocket-money.

We should reward these tough old humans for surviving,
Not with a manager's soggy handshake
Or a medal shaped like an alarm clock —
No, make them a bit rich,
Give the freedom they always heard about
When the bloody chips were down
And the blitz or the desert
Swallowed their friends.
Retire, retire into a fungus basement
Where nothing moves except the draught
And the light and dark grey figures
Doubling their money on the screen;
Where the cabbages taste like the mummy's hand
And the meat tastes of feet;
Where there is nothing to say except:
'Remember?' or 'Your turn to dust the cat'.

To hell with retiring. Let them advance.
Give them the money they've always earned
Or more — and let them choose.
If Mr Burley wants to be a miser,
Great, let the moneybags sway and clink for him,
Pay him a pillowful of best doubloons.
So Mrs Wells has always longed to travel?
Print her a season ticket to the universe,
Let her slum-white skin
Be tanned by a dozen different planets.
We could wipe away some of their worry,
Some of their pain — what I mean
Is so bloody simple:
The old people are being robbed
And punished and we ought
To be letting them out of their cages
Into green spaces of enchanting light.

ADRIAN MITCHELL

a What does Adrian Mitchell think about the way old people are treated?

b Do you agree with him? (Don't just say 'Yes' or 'No'; say why you agree or disagree.)

c Explain, in your own words, what the poet is saying in the first verse of the poem.

d What does the word 'fungus' suggest about the basement? (line 13)

e Who are 'the light and dark grey figures'? (line 15)

f How much money does Adrian Mitchell believe old people should be given?

g What are 'doubloons'? (line 26)

h What do you think 'slum-white skin' is? (line 20)

i What word is used in the last verse to describe the places where old people live?

j Find another word that might be used instead of 'enchanting'. (line 37)

k Look back at the statistics of old people in Britain and at Adrian Mitchell's poem.

l In what ways do you think the poem adds to what we can learn from the statistics?

OLD PEOPLE IN BRITAIN

People old enough to draw a pension number about 10 million and the number is still rising.

The basic rate pension is under 20 per cent of what an average man earns; £10 for every £50.

More than 40 per cent of people over 75 do not have children to share any part of their life with.

Nearly half the people aged 85 and over cannot walk down the road on their own.

Nearly 10 per cent of pensioners live in homes without their own bath or inside toilet.

Beautiful Old Age

It ought to be lovely to be old
to be full of the peace that comes of experience
and wrinkled ripe fulfilment.

The wrinkled smile of completeness that follows a life
lived undaunted and unsoured with accepted lies.
If people lived without accepting lies
they would ripen like apples, and be scented like pippins
in their old age.

Soothing, old people should be, like apples
when one is tired of love.
Fragrant like yellowing leaves, and dim with the soft
stillness and satisfaction of autumn.

And a girl should say:
It must be wonderful to live and grow old.
Look at my mother, how rich and still she is!—

And a young man should think: By Jove
my father has faced all weathers, but it's been a life!—

D. H. LAWRENCE

In Oak Terrace

Old and alone, she sits at nights,
nodding before the television.
The house is quiet now. She knits,
rises to put the kettle on,

watches a cowboy's killing, reads
the local Births and Deaths, and falls
asleep at 'Growing stock-piles of war-heads'.
A world that threatens worse ills

fades. She dreams of life spent
in the one house: suffers again
poverty, sickness, abandonment,
a child's death, a brother's brain

melting to madness. Seventy years
of common trouble; the kettle sings.
At midnight she says her silly prayers,
and takes her teeth out, and collects her night-things.

TONY CONNOR

How I wish my eyesight was better so I could knit as I used to.

How lucky I am that friends and neighbours call and see me and do my shopping on bad days.

I wish I could get my breath when the winds are cold.

How lucky I am to have my own home and still go upstairs in spite of my sciatica.

How I wish my family came more often - I'm so lonely.

How lucky I am that I can still see to read and watch television.

How I wish I was my own boss and in my old home.

How lucky I am to get letters from friends who care.

How I wish these old legs could take me where I would like to go.

How lucky I am to have many happy memories and people who call for a chat.

A Day in the Life ...

Can you put together a picture of a day in the life of an old person?

Think of the old people that you know personally.

Have a good look at the poems.

Read the extracts which show what a couple of old people think and feel.

Try to imagine which jobs are most difficult.

How do you think the day is filled up?

What memories might there be?

You can write this as a description or imagining that you are the old person.

Geriatric Ward

Feeding time in the geriatric ward;
I wondered how they found their mouths,
and seeing that not one looked up, inquired
'Do they have souls?'

'If I had a machine-gun,' answered the doctor
'I'd show you dignity in death instead of living death.
Death wasn't meant to be kept alive.
But we're under orders
to pump blood and air in after the mind's gone.
I don't understand souls;
I only learned about cells
law-abiding as leaves
withering under frost.
But we, never handing over
to Mother who knows best,
spray cabbages with oxygen, hoping for a smile,
count pulses of breathing bags whose direction is lost,
and think we've won.

Here's a game you can't win —
One by one they ooze away in the cold.
There's no society forbidding
this dragged-out detention of the old.'

PHOEBE HESKETH

28

The first line of the poem is about a hospital; what else does it remind you of?

What does the doctor want to do?

How does he describe the old people in the second verse?

What does the last line of the poem make the hospital sound like?

What do you think of the doctor's attitude?

HOSPITAL VISITS

6 She didn't look like my nan lying there. At first I wouldn't even go near the bed. 9

6 It seemed really funny to see my older sister, propped up on pillows holding a baby. 'You're an uncle now', she said. That made me feel as if I was at least 40 years old. 9

6 We went through the main swing doors and my mother had a word with a porter. We turned to the right and walked for what seemed like miles. My feet echoed on the hard floors and I thought how every bit of the hospital we passed through looked the same as the last. 9

6 Everything was bright, white and clean and the nurses smiled at you. But it wasn't like home. 9

6 I thought she'd be really miserable after the operation but instead she was bouncing up and down in bed like an out-of-control spring. She said she'd made dozens of new friends and didn't seem very interested in coming home. 9

6 I knew he wouldn't look very nice after the accident. What I wasn't ready for were all the tubes they'd attached to him. He looked as if he were part of some horrible experiment. 9

6 The whole place smelt like school toilets do on the rare occasions when someone has bothered to clean them. By the time I'd been there 30 seconds, I felt sick. 9

Take a good look at both 'Geriatric Ward' and 'The Inheritor' (overleaf).

How do you see hospitals? Try to write in a way that brings to life the sights, sounds, smells and feelings that a hospital creates.

The Inheritor

It has come to this
A boy in a bed
Trailing tubes
Fighting for life

It has come to this
The midnight trysts
When Arthur ruled
Generations of love
Have come to this
A boy in a bed
With a modified heart
Good for life
If he lasts this night

It has come to this
The skill of men
With surgical truths
At their fingertips
It has come to this
The primitive zeal
Of men who crouched
In fetid caves
And cheated night
With their fiery craft
It has come to this
The march of man.

It has come to this
A boy in a bed.
My son, my son,
Inheritor.

HERBERT WILLIAMS

Brain Damaged

Nights were always the worst.
He used to cry out
at frequent intervals —
wild, inhuman sounds
compounded of nothing we
    could comprehend.

And every time I would go to him
in case — just this once —
he might have need of comforting . . .

But, alien at the cot's end,
he would stand and stare
at his own stark world
which I could not enter.

MARGOT STEWART

trysts: pre-arranged meetings
fetid: stinking

30

Pneumoconiosis

This is the Dust;
black diamond dust.
I had thirty years in it, boy,
a laughing red mouth
coming up to spit smuts black
into a handkerchief.

But it's had forty years
in me now;
so fine
you could inhale it
through a gag.
I'll die with it now.
It's in me,
like my blued scars.

But I try not to think about it.

I take things pretty easy, these days;
one step at a time.
Especially the stairs,
I try not to think about it.

I saw my own brother: rising,
dying in panic, gasping
worse than a hooked carp
drowning in air.
Every breath was his last
till the last.

I try not to think about it.

Know me by my slow step,
the occasional little cough, involuntary
and delicate as a consumptive's,
and my lungs full of budgerigars.

DUNCAN BUSH

a   Who do you think is speaking this poem?

b   Why does he 'take things pretty easy, these days'?

c   What is 'black diamond dust'?

d   What does 'coming up' mean?

e   How does the man feel about his situation?

f   From what you learn in the poem, try to describe what it's like to have pneumoconiosis.

g   How can you work out that the man is retired?

h   What do you think the poem's last line means?

Pneumoconiosis: the progressive damage to the lungs caused by working conditions

The Gresford Disaster

You've heard of the Gresford disaster,
The terrible price that was paid;
Two hundred and forty-two colliers were lost
And three men of a rescue brigade.

It occurred in the month of September;
At three in the morning that pit
Was wracked by a violent explosion
In the Dennis where dust lay so thick.

The gas in the Dennis deep section
Was packed like snow in a drift,
And many a man had to leave the coal-face
Before he had worked out his shift.

A fortnight before the explosion
To the shot-firer, Tomlinson cried:
'If you fire that shot we'll be all blown to hell!'
And no one can say that he lied.

The fireman's reports they are missing,
The records of forty-two days,
The colliery manager had them destroyed
To cover his criminal ways.

Down there in the dark they are lying,
They died for nine shillings a day;
They've worked out their shift and it's now they must lie
In the darkness until Judgement Day.

The Lord Mayor of London's collecting
To help both the children and wives.
The owners had sent some white lilies
To pay for the colliers' lives.

Farewell our dear wives and our children,
Farewell our dear comrades as well.
Don't send your sons in the dark dreary mine
They'll be damned like the sinners in Hell.

ANON.

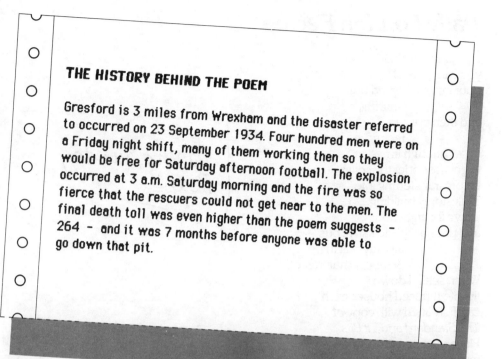

THE HISTORY BEHIND THE POEM

Gresford is 3 miles from Wrexham and the disaster referred
to occurred on 23 September 1934. Four hundred men were on
a Friday night shift, many of them working then so they
would be free for Saturday afternoon football. The explosion
occurred at 3 a.m. Saturday morning and the fire was so
fierce that the rescuers could not get near to the men. The
final death toll was even higher than the poem suggests –
264 – and it was 7 months before anyone was able to
go down that pit.

Sometimes, when people want to look carefully at a poem, they forget the simple
things. One of the most obvious ways to study a poem is to look at what is said in each
individual verse (or stanza).

Each verse in 'The Gresford Disaster' tells us a little bit more about the tragedy.

Write down for yourself what you discover verse by verse.

When you've done that, you'll see that you've said far more about the poem than you
would have done if someone had simply asked you, 'What's the poem about?'

Two more poems that are made easier to understand in this way are 'The Hayes,
Cardiff' (on page 91) and 'Travelling through the Dark' (on page 60). Try looking at
them as well in this way.

Daily London Recipe

Take any number of them
you can think of,
pour into empty red bus
                until full,
and then push in
                ten more.
Allow enough time
to get hot under the collar
before transferring into
multistorey building.
Leave for eight hours,
and pour back into same bus
                already half full.
                Scrape remainder off.
When settled down
tip into terraced houses each
carefully lined with copy of
The Standard and *Tit Bits*.
Place mixture before open
television screen at 7 p.m.
and then allow to cool
in bed at 10.30 p.m.
May be served with
working overalls
or pinstripe suit.

                STEVE TURNER

Boring Sunday Recipe

Christmas Recipe

Stuff one oversized turkey
Then pour everyone a large glass of

Rugby Team Recipe

Hit Record Recipe

Take one good-looking singer
(Need not be able to sing the right notes)
Hire a studio for

Exam Recipe

Take any number of useless facts
Find a class of empty brains
And start cramming the

Newspaper Recipe

Find a pile of gossip
Add some pretty girls
And the occasional piece of news
Stir the whole

Daily School Recipe

Take one very loud bell system
And make it ring every 40 minutes
Train pupils to push chairs anywhere
And run when bell

Holiday Recipe

Write your own piece in the form of a recipe, using one of the subjects suggested or taking another subject of your own choice.

This is quite difficult to do well, so you would do best to work on rough paper at the beginning.

Once you've got a blank piece of paper in front of you and can't think of a single word to put down, ask yourself this question: what things go to make up my subject? For example, if you've chosen 'Boring Sunday Recipe', ask yourself what ingredients make Sunday a really boring day?

If your recipe turns out to be relatively brief, you'll have time to try your hand at a second, and maybe more.

Song of the Wagondriver

My first love was the ten-ton truck
they gave me when I started,
and though she played the bitch with me
I grieved when we were parted.

Since then I've had a dozen more,
the wound was quick to heal,
and now it's easier to say
I'm married to my wheel.

I've trunked it north, I've trunked it south,
on wagons good and bad,
but none were ever really like
the first I ever had.

The life is hard, the hours are long,
sometimes I cease to feel,
but I go on, for it seems to me
I'm married to my wheel.

Often I think of my home and kids,
out on the road at night,
and think of taking a local job
provided the money's right.

Two nights a week I see my wife,
and eat a decent meal,
but otherwise, for all my life,
I'm married to my wheel.

B. S. JOHNSON

A Danish Pastry Lament

She was a silver haired goddess,
a gift from heaven,
she worked at Cadbury's
got up at seven.

She was a silk skin wonder,
a vintage wine,
always in work by
a quarter to nine.

She was my Christmas stocking,
my piece in our time,
a classic poem,
my very own crime.

She was the cake of my fancy,
I held our love dear
as we danced through the gateaux
past the chocolate eclairs.

She ran off with the milkman
on a day long gone,
she fell for his yoghurt
and evil was done.

She was a silver haired goddess,
a song in the night,
but now I have lost
my angel delight.

STEWART HENDERSON

A Working Mum

From morning, till night,
Life is one maddening rush.
The alarm bell rings,
You awake to a fuss.
Jump from your bed, to fight,
For a place on the bus.
Someone, who had stood
Close behind you,
Now you discover
Is in front of the queue.

You don't want trouble.
So what do you do?
You stand there fuming,
The bus draws alongside,
A quick kick on her heel
Now you're climbing inside.
You smile at the conductor,
It's just made your day,
She's still looking around her
While the bus draws away.

You arrive in work
At the stroke of nine,
You clock your card
The weather is fine.
You smile all around,
'Good Morning' to you.
Then a voice in your ear
Bawls, 'Have you nothing to do?'
You sit down quickly,
You have laddered your tights.

Seems today you have
Nothing but frights.
You keep your head down,
You daren't look up.
The hooter blows,
You run for a cup.
The canteen is full,
Back in the queue.
You wait so long,
The hooter's just blew.

Though you feel thirsty
You have to get back,
If you dawdle too long
You will get the sack.
So you rush and you pant
Till you get through the day.
There goes the hooter,
You're now on your way.
You join the bus queue,
The one at the top,

The bus is full,
It won't even stop
You are hungry and cold,
You've had a long day.
No wonder your hair
Shows steaks of grey.
You have made it at last,
There is the gate.
Time for a cuppa?
'Mum, why are you late?'

SALLY FLOOD

A WORKING LIFE?

Everyone claims that they're far too busy, but is it true?

See if you can find out how your day compares with that of an adult you know.

(The most obvious choice is a parent or an older brother or sister but the decision is up to you.)

Set your findings out as a **work chart**.

It might look a little like this...

Myself		My Brother Sid	
7:55	Woken up	7:30	Gets up
8:05	Woken up again	7:45	Breakfast
8.15	Kicked out of bed	8:10	Bus to work
8:25	Breakfast	8:30	Supposed to start work
8:30	Catch bus to school	8:40-ish	Starts work
8.45	In playground	10:30	Coffee break
8:55	Registration	10:45	More work

Your chart and your conversations in preparing that chart should give you plenty of material to write a discussion piece called

WORK: IS IT A FOUR LETTER WORD?

It's up to you how you do it but you could comment on these areas

- the time people spend on work
- different types of work
- attitudes to work
- the work that teachers do
- the ways you can avoid work
- part-time jobs
- housework
- the money people earn for the work they do

Meditation on the A30

A man on his own in a car
    Is revenging himself on his wife;
He opens the throttle and bubbles with dottle
    And puffs at his pitiful life.

'She's losing her looks very fast,
    She loses her temper all day;
That lorry won't let me get past,
    This Mini is blocking my way.

'Why can't you step on it and shift her!
    I can't go on crawling like this!
At breakfast she said that she wished I was dead—
    Thank heavens we don't have to kiss.

'I'd like a nice blonde on my knee
    And one who won't argue or nag.
Who dares to coming hooting at *me?*
    I only give way to a Jag.

'You're barmy or plastered, I'll pass you, you bastard—
    I will overtake you. *I will!*'
As he clenches his pipe, his moment is ripe
    And the corner's accepting its kill.

JOHN BETJEMAN

Quiet Fun

My son Augustus, in the street, one day,
    Was feeling quite exceptionally merry.
A stranger asked him: 'Can you tell me, pray,
    The quickest way to Brompton Cemetery?'
'The quickest way? You bet I can!' said Gus,
    And pushed the fellow underneath a bus.

*   *   *

Whatever people say about my son,
He does enjoy his little bit of fun.

HARRY GRAHAM

42

In the Cemetery

'You see those mothers squabbling there?'
Remarks the man of the cemetery.
'One says in tears, *"Tis mine lies here!"*
Another, *"Nay, mine, you Pharisee!"*
Another, *"How dare you move my flowers
And put your own on this grave of ours!"*
But all their children were laid therein
At different times, like sprats in a tin.

'And then the main drain had to cross,
And we moved the lot some nights ago,
And packed them away in the general foss
With hundreds more. But their folks don't know,
And as well cry over a new-laid drain
As anything else, to ease your pain!'

THOMAS HARDY

Pharisee: used here to mean a person who
         says one thing while he/she knows
         the truth to be quite different
   foss: trench

Notting Hill Polka

We've—had—
A Body in the house
   Since father passed away:
He took bad on
Saturday night an' he
   Went the followin' day.

Mum's—pulled—
The blinds all down
   An' bought some Sherry Wine,
An' we've put the tin
What the Arsenic's in
   At the bottom of the Ser-pen-tine!

W. BRIDGES-ADAM

Ianto the Undertaker

Ianto undertakes by trade, though only assistant
these long years to John Mawr. Short and swarthy,
Iberian Ianto embalms the dead, loves his trade.
'It's bloody good mun,' he said to me,
in undertones so that John wouldn't hear,
'it's a good living, this looking after the dead.'

He told me of the way the corpses contract,
creak and coil after death; of the way
that cries break from bodies now without breath.
'Don't tell John Mawr,' he said furtively,
'but there's some good pickings, too, you see,
for the families often leave gold rings
on the fingers of the dead –
but I get them before they go down the hole!'
'But how do you manage to remove the rings,'
I questioned, 'with the fingers so stiff and swollen?'
'Simple boy,' he said with pride, 'they *are* stiff,
I admit, but I just break the bloody fingers
clean off, see – snap them like carrots I do!
Would you like to see my collection of wedding rings?'
I declined, and he continued, eager to tell,
'the job's got a good future, you know,
there's no slumps in this trade; constant it is.'
He turned back to work on his treasured coffins then,
and I walked down Llangarw's narrow main street,
seeing for a moment his black-nailed hands
scurrying like furred spiders
over the slow rictus of the fading dead flesh.

BRYN GRIFFITHS

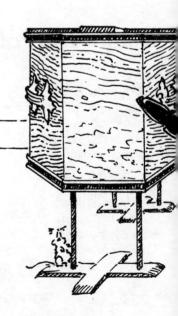

Iberian: Spanish
   rictus: death grin

You've got to *hear* this poem to get the most out of it. Of course, it's best done with a Welsh valleys accent but it's worth trying it with whatever accents are available. It works well if one person reads Ianto's words and another reads the rest of the poem. Try it, if you can, with a number of accents. Which ones work best?

Could you do Ianto's job?

What about working down a sewer?

Would you be any good at changing nappies?

Or cleaning up sick?

What about working in a laboratory with rats or mice?

Or letting a spider crawl across your flesh?

Or camping in an area where there are snakes?

Choose the most stomach-churning situation that you could imagine yourself in and write about it as if you were there.

Epitaphs

(You know, the things you read on graves!)

For a dentist

Stranger! Approach this spot with gravity!

John Brown is filling his last cavity.

Anna

The children of Israel wanted bread

The Lord he sent them manna

But this good man he wanted a wife

And the Devil sent him Anna.

What do you think people might write about you after you've gone? What would you be remembered for?

Don't worry whether it rhymes or not. Just see if you can work out three or four lines that someone might write about you when you're no longer here.

If you're stuck for a beginning, a lot of epitaphs start 'Here lies ...'

Once you've done one for yourself, see if you can produce something similar for two or three of your friends.

Will their epitaph remember something about them as a person or something they did? It's up to you.

Passport

He passed the copper without any fuss,
And he passed the cart of hay,
He tried to pass a swerving bus
And then he passed away.

From Devon

Here lies a man who was killed by lightning;
He died when his prospects seemed to be brightening.
He might have cut a flash in this world of trouble,
But the flash cut him, and he lies in the stubble.

Freedom

(Holloway, Spring 1969)

Here at least, I thought,
I shall find freedom.
Here in prison all encumbrances
will be removed.
I shall be left without the burden of
possessions, responsibilities, relationships.
Alone and naked I shall feel
a fresh wind over my entire uncluttered body
blow each pore clear,
cooling and cleaning every crevice.

At last I shall know the relief of
simply obeying orders,
owning nothing,
caring for no-one,
being uncared for.

I shall sit content for hours on end
in a bare cell,
glad to be cut off from
things, people, commitments and the
confusing world outside.

But I was wrong.
There is no freedom here—
prison is the world in microcosm.

In my locker is a cache of valuables:
needle, cotton, nail-file, pencil.
My wages buy me fruit and biscuits which
I hoard and hide,
fearing they'll get stolen.

Meticulously I arrange the flowers that
outside friends send in;
carefully decorate my cell with cut out pictures;
get flustered if I lose my mug or bucket.

I am no hermit from the outside world,
but strain through busy days to read
each item in the newspapers.
International problems follow me inside;
a prisoner is picked on—she is coloured.

Every evening I am forced to choose
between a range of recreations:
I may read or dance or take a bath,
go to class, play darts or
watch the news.

I am seldom on my own:
a geometry of love, hate, friendship
forms about me.
Someone calls my name,
enters my cell,
asks a favour,
makes some claim upon me.

And I marvel
as I lie alone at night
that this world is as complex as the other;
that even here in jail I am not free to
lose my freedom.

PAT ARROWSMITH

a   How do you think you would feel if you were about to be put in prison?

b   Why did Pat Arrowsmith actually expect to be happy in jail?

c   Explain what each of these words mean as they are used in the poem:

(i)   encumbrances (line 3)
(ii)   crevice (line 10)
(iii) meticulously (line 29)
(iv)   flustered (line 32)
(v)   hermit (line 33)

(Even if you don't know the words, you can make intelligent guesses by reading carefully the sentences in which the words are found.)

d   What example does Pat Arrowsmith give to show that the prison is very much like the wider world outside?

e   In a paragraph of your own, describe prison life as Pat Arrowsmith experienced it. (Don't simply imagine it, use the poem to find out!)

f   Make a list of the things you would miss if you were in prison. At the end of the list say which things you would miss most of all and explain why.

Parents' Sayings

You're old enough to wash your own socks.

He's not coming through that door again, I can tell you.

If it's true what your teacher said then you can say goodbye to
   that coat we were going to get you.

You do it and like it.

When did you last wash your feet?

Why don't you do a Saturday job?

The answer's NO.

The biscuits are for *everyone* – OK?

Don't mind me, I'm just your mother.

You haven't ridden that bike of yours for years.

You try and leave home and I'll chuck you out on your ear.

You're certainly not going to put that up on any wall in this
   house.

Do you know what a Hoover is?

You can pay for the next phone bill.

If you don't like this caff – find another one.

Just 'cos he's doing biology he thinks he's going to be a brain
   surgeon.

Do you remember that lovely Christmas when he was six?

MICHAEL ROSEN

Of course, parents never really say things like that . . . do they?

Well, perhaps just sometimes.

What do your family say?

The phrase that sticks in my mind is: 'I'll count to three—One, two . . . ' You hardly ever heard three because the consequences of not doing what you were told within three seconds were too horrible to think about.

In trying to remember the phrases that parents use, it might be helpful to think about the situations when the conversation gets interesting. Here are some possibilities:

getting up in the morning
at meal times
visiting relatives
watching television
clearing up your bedroom
getting to school on time
doing homework
getting home too late at night
helping with housework
your choice of friends

To prepare your own Parents' Sayings, it's probably best to write as many as you can down in rough first and then put them into a suitable order.

(They don't simply have to be what your parents say. As long as they sound true, use them.)

Poor but Honest

(An old music hall song, author unknown)

She was poor, but she was honest,
    Victim of the squire's whim:
First he loved her, then he left her,
    And she lost her honest name.

Then she ran away to London,
    For to hide her grief and shame;
There she met another squire,
    And she lost her name again.

See her riding in her carriage,
    In the Park and all so gay:
All the nibs and nobby persons
    Come to pass the time of day.

See the little old-world village
    Where her aged parents live,
Drinking the champagne she sends them;
    But they never can forgive.

In the rich man's arms she flutters,
    Like a bird with broken wing:
First he loved her, then he left her,
    And she hasn't got a ring.

See him in the splendid mansion,
    Entertaining with the best,
While the girl that he has ruined,
    Entertains a sordid guest.

See him in the House of Commons,
    Making laws to put down crime,
While the victim of his passions
    Trails her way through mud and slime.

Standing on the bridge at midnight,
    She says: 'Farewell, blighted Love.'
There's a scream, a splash—Good Heavens!
    What is she a-doing of?

Then they dragged her from the river,
    Water from her clothes they wrang,
For they thought that she was drownded;
    But the corpse got up and sang:

'It's the same the whole world over;
    It's the poor that gets the blame,
It's the rich that get the pleasure.
    Isn't it a blooming shame?'

The Ruined Maid

'O' Melia, my dear, this does everything crown!
Who could have supposed I should meet you in Town?
And whence such fair garments, such prosperi-ty?' —
'O didn't you know I'd been ruined?' said she.

—'At home in the barton you said "thee" and "thou",
And "thik oon", and "theäs oon", and "t'other"; but now
Your talking quite fits 'ee for high compa-ny!' —
'Some polish is gained with one's ruin,' said she.

—'At home in the barton you said "thee" and "thou",
And "thik oon", and "theäs oon", and "t'other"; but now
Your talking quite fits 'ee for high compa-ny!' —
'Some polish is gained with one's ruin,' said she.

—'Your hands were like paws then, your face blue and bleak
But now I'm bewitched by your delicate cheek,
And your little gloves fit as on any la-dy!' —
'We never do work when we're ruined,' said she.

—'You used to call home-life a hag-ridden dream,
And you'd sigh, and you'd sock; but at present you seem
To know not of megrims or melancho-ly!' —
'True. One's pretty lively when ruined,' said she.

—'I wish I had feathers, a fine sweeping gown,
And a delicate face, and could strut about Town!' —
'My dear — a raw country girl, such as you be,
Cannot quite expect that. You ain't ruined,' said she.

THOMAS HARDY

An old friend meets you a couple of years after
you've left home to seek your fortune.

Write out the conversation that you have.

Nice Men

I know a nice man who is kind to his wife and always lets her
   do what she wants.

I heard of another man who killed his girlfriend. It was
   an accident. He pushed her in a quarrel and she split open
   her skull on the dining-room table. He was such a
   guilt-ridden sight in court that the jury felt sorry for him.

My friend Aiden is nice. He thinks women are really equal.

There are lots of nice men who help their wives with the
   shopping and the housework.

And many men, when you are alone with them, say, 'I prefer
   women. They are so understanding.' This is another
   example of men being nice.

Some men, when you make a mistake at work, just laugh.
   They don't go on about it or shout. That's nice.

At times, the most surprising men will say at parties, 'There's
   a lot to this Women's Lib.' Here, again, is a case of men
   behaving in a nice way.

Another nice thing is that some men are sympathetic when
   their wives feel unhappy.
I've often heard men say, 'Don't worry about everything so
   much, dear.'

You hear stories of men who are far more than nice – putting
   women in lifeboats first, etc.

Sometimes when a man has not been nice, he apologises and
   trusts you with intimate details of the pressures in his life.
   This just shows how nice he is, underneath.

I think that is all I can say on the subject of nice men. Thank
   you.

DOROTHY BYRNE

See if you can write a piece to go with Dorothy Byrne's poem called 'Nice Girls'.

For example: what sort of music do 'nice girls' listen to?
                  what television do they watch?

what about eating and drinking?
how do they get on with their family?
what do they read?
what are their hobbies?
what about their clothes? their boy friends?

If you're not sure how to start, here are three possibilities:
'Nice girls keep diaries and tell their mothers everything'
'Nice girls write long letters and never forget birthdays'
'Nice girls dance with each other around a pile of handbags'

MR AVERAGE

... weighs 11 stone 8 pounds

... has a bath three times a week

... will earn enough in 8 minutes to buy a loaf of bread

... will throw away the equivalent of six trees in his
rubbish bin each year.

... will drink more beer than milk

... will weigh himself once a year

... will drink 260 glasses of wine and 52 glasses of
spirits in a year

... stands 5 feet 8 and a half inches high

... will eat approximately 200 eggs, 250 pounds of
vegetables and 50 pounds of sugar every year

... will have to work for 2 hours to have enough money
for a bottle of whisky

...will brush his teeth for only twenty seconds a day

(At least, that is what the statisticians say.)

A Girl's Song

Early one morning
As I went out walking
I saw the young sailor
Go fresh through the fields.
His eye was as blue as
The sky up above us
And clean was his skin
As the colour of shells.

O where are you going,
Young sailor, so early?
And may I come with you
A step as you go?
He looked with his eye
And I saw the deep sea-tombs,
He opened his mouth
And I heard the sea roar.

And limp on his head
Lay his hair green as sea-grass
And scrubbed were his bones
By the inching of sand.
The long tides enfolded
The lines of his body
And slow corals grow
At the stretch of his hand.

I look from my window
In the first light of morning
And I look from my door
At the dark of the day,
But all that I see are
The fields flat and empty
And the black road run down
To Cardigan town.

LESLIE NORRIS

Hedgehog

Twitching the leaves just where the drainpipe clogs
In ivy leaves and mud, a purposeful
Creature at night about its business. Dogs
Fear his stiff seriousness. He chews away

At beetles, worms, slugs, frogs. Can kill a hen
With one snap of his jaws, can taunt a snake
To death on muscled spines. Old countrymen
Tell tales of hedgehogs sucking a cow dry.

But this one, cramped by houses, fences, walls,
Must have slept here all winter in that heap
Of compost, or have inched by intervals
Through tidy gardens to this ivy bed.

And here, dim-eyed, but ears so sensitive
A voice within the house can make him freeze,
He scuffs the edge of danger; yet can live
Happily in our nights and absences.

A country creature, wary, quiet and shrewd,
He takes the milk we give him, when we're gone.
At night, our slamming voices must seem crude
To one who sits and waits for silences.

ANTHONY THWAITE

Our Budgie

Our budgie lives in a cage of wire
Equipped to please his each desire,
He has a little ladder to climb
And he's up and down it all the time.
And a little mirror in which he peeps
As he utters his self-admiring cheeps,
And two little pink plastic budgie mates
Whom he sometimes loves and sometimes hates.
And a little bell all made of tin
On which he makes a merry din.
Though sometimes, when things aren't going well,
He hides his head inside the bell.
His feathers are a brilliant green
And take most of his time to preen,
His speech is limited and blurred
But he doesn't do badly, for a bird.
And though he can but poorly talk
If you ignore him he'll squawk and squawk
And fly into a fearful rage
And rattle the bars of his pretty cage,
But he won't get out, he'll never try it,
And a cloth on the cage will keep him quiet.

This futile bird, it seems to me,
Would make a perfect Welsh MP.

PS to the above
Despite his repertoire of tricks
Poor budgie died in 1966.

HARRI WEBB

a What is there in the budgie's cage that can make the budgie's life more contented?

b What is a 'din'?

c What is the budgie doing when he decides to 'preen' himself?

d What is a 'repertoire' of tricks?

e Suggest two ways in which the budgie might be like an MP
(... if we believe the poet!)

f What sort of tone is the writer using in this poem?

g Perhaps animals would be better suited to a number of the jobs more normally done by humans. For example, gorillas seem ideally fitted to do jobs as door-to-door salesmen. They'd be able to carry large heavy suitcases without any problem and who in their right mind would refuse a gorilla who was standing on their doorstep?

Choose an animal for each of the jobs mentioned below and say why you think it might be good at the job. (If you've got time you can add further ideas of your own.)

magistrate	nurse	social worker
traffic warden	secretary	insurance salesman
air hostess	electrician	shop assistant

Travelling through the Dark

Travelling through the dark I found a deer
dead on the edge of the Wilson River road.
It is usually best to roll them into the canyon:
that road is narrow; to swerve might make more dead.

By glow of the taillight I stumbled back of the car
and stood by the heap, a doe, a recent killing;
she had stiffened already, almost cold.
I dragged her off; she was large in the belly.

My fingers touching her side brought me the reason –
her side was warm; her fawn lay there waiting,
alive, still, never to be born.
Beside that mountain road I hesitated.

The car aimed ahead its lowered parking lights;
under the hood purred the steady engine.
I stood in the glare of the warm exhaust turning red;
around our group I could hear the wilderness listen.

I thought hard for us all – my only swerving –
then pushed her over the edge into the river.

WILLIAM STAFFORD

Death of a Cat

I rose early
On the fourth day
Of his illness,
And went downstairs
To see if he was
All right.

He was not in the
House, and I rushed
Wildly round the
Garden calling his name.

I found him lying
Under a rhododendron
Bush,
His black fur
Wet, and matted
With the dew.

I knelt down beside him.
And he opened his
Mouth as if to
Miaow
But no sound came.

I picked him up
And he lay quietly
In my arms
As I carried him
Indoors.

Suddenly he gave
A quiet miaow
And I felt his body tense,
And then lie still.

I laid his warm,
Lifeless body on
The floor, and
Rubbed my fingers
Through his fur.

A warm tear
Dribbled down
My cheek and
Left a salt taste
On my lips.

I stood up, and
Walked quietly
Out of the room.

ANTHONY THOMPSON

A Case of Murder

They should not have left him alone,
Alone that is except for the cat.
He was only nine, not old enough
To be left alone in a basement flat,
5   Alone, that is, except for the cat.
A dog would have been a different thing,
A big gruff dog with slashing jaws,
But a cat with round eyes mad as gold,
Plump as a cushion with tucked-in paws —
10 Better have left him with a fair-sized rat!
But what they did was leave him with a cat.
He hated that cat; he watched it sit,
A buzzing machine of soft black stuff,
He sat and watched and he hated it,
15 Snug in its fur, hot blood in a muff,
And its mad gold stare and the way it sat
Crooning dark warmth: he loathed all that.
So he took Daddy's stick and he hit the cat.
Then quick as a sudden crack in glass
20 It hissed, black flash, to a hiding place
In the dust and dark beneath the couch,
And he followed the grin on his new-made face,
A wide-eyed, frightened snarl of a grin,
And he took the stick and he thrust it in,
25 Hard and quick in the furry dark,
The black fur squealed and he felt his skin
Prickle with sparks of dry delight.
Then the cat again came into sight,
Shot for the door that wasn't quite shut,
30 But the boy, quick too, slammed fast the door:
The cat, half-through, was cracked like a nut
And the soft black thud was dumped on the floor.
Then the boy was suddenly terrified
And he bit his knuckles and cried and cried;
35 But he had to do something with the dead thing there.
His eyes squeezed beads of salty prayer
But the wound of fear gaped wide and raw;
He dared not touch the thing with his hands
So he fetched a spade and shovelled it
40 And dumped the load of heavy fur
In the spidery cupboard under the stair
Where it's been for years, and though it died
It's grown in that cupboard and its hot low purr
Grows slowly louder year by year:
45 There'll not be a corner for the boy to hide
When the cupboard swells and all sides split
And the huge black cat pads out of it.

VERNON SCANNELL

62

a   What was your immediate reaction to this poem?

b   How old is the boy?

c   Why would a dog have been all right with the boy?

d   Find other words that might be used instead of
(i) gruff (line 7), (ii) snug (line 15).

e   How does the boy kill the cat?

f   Describe the cat as fully as you can. (If you use phrases from the poem, try to explain what they mean.)

g   After the death what does the boy do which suggests he is afraid?

h   What is meant by: 'His eyes squeezed beads of salty prayer' (line 36)?

i   Write your own story in which something horrible is done and in which the evil eventually catches up with the person or people involved. (You may well find it best to write as if you or your friends were the people in the story.)

A YEAR IN THE LIFE OF THE RSPCA

Telephone calls recieved	1,003.045
Animals treated	188,279
Animals humanely destroyed	141,381

(This includes 44,668 cats and dogs that were too sick or too injured to live and 17,136 unwanted newborn puppies and kittens.)

New homes found	111,300
Complaints received about animal cruelty	47,362
Convictions obtained for animal cruelty	1,889

(In 22 cases prison sentences were imposed and in another 11 cases there were suspended prison sentences.)

Disqualifications from keeping animals following court cases	429

(NB RSPCA = Royal Society for the Prevention of Cruelty to Animals. The figures quoted are for 1984.)

The Dog Lovers

So they bought you
And kept you in a
Very good home
Central heating
TV
A deep freeze
A *very* good home –
No one to take you
For that lovely long run –
But otherwise
'A *very* good home'.
They fed you Pal and Chum
But not that lovely long run,
Until, mad with energy and boredom
You escaped – and ran and ran and ran
Under a car.
Today they will cry for you –
Tomorrow they will buy another dog.

SPIKE MILLIGAN

64

Song of the Battery Hen

We can't grumble about accommodation:
We have a new concrete floor that's
Always dry, four walls that are
Painted white, and sheet-iron roof
The rain drums on. A fan blows warm air
Beneath our feet to disperse the smell
Of chickenshit and, on dull days,
Fluorescent lighting sees us.

You can tell me: if you come by
The North door, I am in the twelfth pen
On the left-hand side of the third row
From the floor; and in that pen
I am usually the middle one of three.
But even without directions, you'd
Discover me. I have the same orange-
Red comb, yellow beak and auburn
Feathers, but as the door opens and you
Hear above the electric fan a kind of
One-word wail, I am the one
Who sounds loudest in my head.

Listen. Outside this house there's an
Orchard with small moss-green apple
Trees; beyond that, two fields of
Cabbages: then, on the far side of
The road, a broiler-house. Listen;
One cockerel grows out of there, as
Tall and proud as the first hour of the sun.
Sometimes I stop calling with the others
To listen, and I wonder if he hears me.
The next time you come here, look for me.
Notice the way I sound inside my head.
God made us all quite differently,
And blessed us with this expensive home.

EDWIN BROCK

Lone Dog

I'm a lean dog, a keen dog, a wild dog and lone,
I'm a rough dog, a tough dog, hunting on my own!
I'm a bad dog, a mad dog, teasing silly sheep;
I love to sit and bay the moon and keep fat souls from sleep.

I'll never be a lap dog, licking dirty feet,
A sleek dog, a meek dog, cringing for my meat.
Not for me the fireside, the well-filled plate,
But shut door and sharp stone and cuff and kick and hate.

Not for me the other dogs, running by my side,
Some have run a short while, but none of them would bide.
O mine is still the lone trail, the hard trail, the best,
Wide wind and wild stars and the hunger of the quest.

IRENE McLEOD

Lying in the grass,
I wait, watch, hiss
At the sound of footsteps.

If they put you behind bars,
It's 2 or 5 or 10 years;
Even a life sentence
Isn't really what it says.
But with me . . .

Who do you think is speaking in these extracts?

Make no mistake about it, I run this house.
They may pay the mortgage,
Buy the furniture,
Lock the door at night,
But I am the one who . . .

Day after day, week after week,
They throw bread to me.
I don't understand it
But I eat it nonetheless
(Except the stale egg sandwiches)

Write your own piece in which an animal has its say.

Vegetarian Verse

I

Mary had a little lamb
She bought it as a trinket
She put it in the liquidiser
So everyone could drink it.

II

Little Jack Horner
Sat in a corner
Eating his veal and ham pie
He pulled out a sliver
Of some mouse's liver
And most of the same mouse's eye.

DAVID BRAZIER

You think these are nasty? You should read some of the real nursery rhymes. What about 'Four and twenty blackbirds *baked* in a pie'? As for 'Three Blind Mice', one animal rights group has tried to ban it from schools on the grounds that it encourages cruelty to animals.

Can you come up with any ideas for adapting a nursery rhyme? For a start, who pushed Humpty Dumpty . . . ?

Killing a Whale

A whale is killed as follows:
A shell is filled with dynamite and
A harpoon takes the shell.
You wait until the great grey back
Breaches the sliding seas, you squint,
Take aim.
The cable snakes like a squirt of paint,
The shell channels deep through fluke
And flank, through mural softness
To bang among the blubber,
Exploding terror through
The hollow fleshy chambers,
While the hooks fly open
Like an umbrella
Gripping the tender tissue.

It dies with some panache,
Whipping the capstan like
A schoolboy's wooden top,
Until the teeth of the machine
Can hold its anger, grip.
Its dead tons thresh for hours
The ravished sea,
Then sink together, sag –
So air is pumped inside
To keep the corpse afloat,
And one of those flags that men
Kill mountains with is stuck
Into this massive death.

Dead whales are rendered down,
Give oil.

DAVID GILL

mural: the internal structure of the body
         of the whale

a   At what moment is the harpoon fired?

b   What makes sure that the harpoon stays inside the whale?

c   What does the whale do after it has been struck by the harpoon?

d   How is the whale kept afloat once it has died?

e   What word in this poem means a dead body?

f   For what reason do men kill whales according to David Gill?

g   Why do you think a flag is stuck into the whale?

h   If you were reading this poem aloud, what tone of voice would you use?

i   Why do you think David Gill wrote this poem?

THE WHALE HARVEST

Every year in the Faroe Islands families go to work to bring in 'the crop'. What makes this harvest different from most others is that the crop is whales.

The harvest begins with the capture of one pilot whale. This one is then used as a kind of bait to lure the others to their death. While there is one whale in distress, the others will not desert it, and so they meet the same fate.

The captured whale is speared just behind the dorsal fin and dragged in agony towards the land. Once it has beached itself in shallow water, a hook is sunk into the live whale's head and used to drag it farther up the beach.

A long razor-sharp knife is then driven in, just behind the blow hole. The knife slashes down, through the flesh and blubber and into the animal's vertebrae. The whale is in such pain that it thrashes violently about and eventually breaks its own weakened spine.

It is very much a family affair and one reporter observed six- and seven-year-olds joining in with the kill. Parents teach their children the art of slaughtering whales by letting them practise on the unborn young which are ripped from the wombs of pregnant female whales.

Look back at David Gill's poem and at the description of killing whales in the Faroe Islands. Which kind of killing seems to you to be the more cruel and why?

Dumb Insolence

I'm big for ten years old
Maybe that's why they get at me

Teachers, parents, cops
Always getting at me

When they get at me

I don't hit em
They can do you for that

I don't swear at em
They can do you for that

I stick my hands in my pockets
And stare at them

And while I stare at them
I think about sick

They call it dumb insolence

They don't like it
But they can't do you for it

I've been done before
They say if I get done again

They'll put me in a home
So I do dumb insolence

ADRIAN MITCHELL

What's the Matter?
or
How to Do Nothing and Lose Everything

Him and her. You can make your own mind up which is 'him' and which is 'her'.

What's the matter?
Nothing.
Something's the matter.
No, it isn't.
Then what are you sulking about?
I'm not sulking.
Well you're not exactly happy, are you?
I'm all right.
You don't look it.
I don't have to show it.
You used to.
So now I don't.
You're telling me.
Yes, I know I'm telling you.
Something's the matter then.
No, it isn't.
Yes, it is.
Well, if you know so much about me
    you don't need me to tell you.
No, I suppose not. I'll be off then. I'll see you
    when I see you.

MICHAEL ROSEN

What do you think is happening here?

What has led up to it?

Imagine that you were one of the characters in this conversation.

Later in the day you meet another friend or friends.

Write your own conversation in which you tell them what happened and they say what they think about it all.

The National Union of Children

NUC has just passed a weighty resolution:
'Unless all parents raise our rate of pay
This action will be taken by our members
(The resolution comes in force today):—

'Noses will not be blown (sniffs are in order),
Bedtime will get preposterously late,
Ice-cream and crisps will be consumed for breakfast,
Unwanted cabbage left upon the plate,

'Earholes and fingernails can't be inspected,
Overtime (known as homework) won't be worked,
Reports from school will all say "Could do better",
Putting bricks back in boxes may be shirked.'

The National Association of Parents

Of course, NAP's answer quickly was forthcoming
(It was a matter of emergency),
It issued to the Press the following statement
(Its Secretary appeared upon TV):—

'True that the so-called Saturday allowance
Hasn't kept pace with prices in the shops,
But neither have, alas, parental wages:
NUC's claim would ruin kind, hard-working Pops.

'Therefore, unless that claim is now abandoned,
Strike action for us, too, is what remains;
In planning for the which we are in process
Of issuing, to all our members, canes.'

ROY FULLER

What would a union of young people have to say if you were in charge of it?

What demands would you make and how would you set them out for maximum effect?

THE YOUNG PERSON'S CHARTER

1. The employment and sacking of teachers shall be the sole responsibility of the pupils.

2. Chewing gum shall be provided by the teacher at the start of every lesson.

3. Jobs shall be provided automatically for all pupils leaving school.

4. All school toilets shall be properly equipped with soft toilet paper.

5. Adults shall be banned from saying 'but'.

6. Pupils will be _ _ _ _ _ _ _ _ _ _ _ _ _ _

Nooligan

I'm a nooligan
don't give a toss
in our class
I'm the boss
(well, one of them)

I'm a nooligan
got a nard 'ead
step out of line
and youre dead
(well, bleedin)

I'm a nooligan
I spray me name
all over town
footballs me game
(well, watchin)

I'm a nooligan
violence is fun
gonna be a nassassin
or a nired gun
(well, a soldier)

ROGER McGOUGH

Atrocities

You told me, in your drunken-boasting mood,
How once you butchered prisoners. That was good!
I'm sure you felt no pity while they stood
Patient and cowed and scared, as prisoners should.

How did you do them in? Come, don't be shy:
You know I love to hear how Germans die,
Downstairs in dug-outs. 'Camerad!' they cry;
Then squeal like stoats when bombs begin to fly.

And you? I know your record. You went sick
When orders looked unwholesome: then, with trick
And lie, you wrangled home. And here you are,
Still talking big and boozing in a bar.

SIEGFRIED SASSOON

Green Beret

He was twelve years old,
and I do not know his name.
The mercenaries took him and his father,
whose name I do not know,
one morning upon the High Plateau.
Green Beret looked down on the frail boy
with the eyes of a hurt animal and thought,
a good fright will make him talk.
He commanded, and the father was taken away
behind the forest's green wall.
'Right kid tell us where they are,
tell us where or your father – dead.'
With eyes now bright and filled with terror
the slight boy said nothing.
'You've got one minute kid', said Green Beret,
'tell us where or we kill father'   .
and thrust his wrist-watch against a face all eyes,
the second-hand turning, jerking on its way.
'OK boy ten seconds to tell us where they are'
In the last instant the silver hand shattered the
     sky and the forest of trees.
'Kill the old guy' roared Green Beret
and shots hammered out
behind the forest's green wall
and sky and trees and soldiers stood
in silence, and the boy cried out.
Green Beret stood
in silence, as the boy crouched down
and shook with tears,
as children do when their father dies.

'Christ', said one mercenary to Green Beret,
'he didn't know a damn thing
we killed the old guy for nothing'
so they all went away.
Green Beret and his mercenaries.

And the boy knew everything.
He knew everything about them, the caves,
the trails the hidden places and the names,
and in the moment that he cried out,
in that same instant,
protected by frail tears
far stronger than any wall of steel,
they passed everywhere
like tigers
across the High Plateau.

HO THIEN

HOW WOULD EACH SIDE REMEMBER THAT DAY?

THE SOLDIER

I didn't want to be there.
There was a job to be done and someone had to do it.
You had to be tough just to survive.

THE BOY

Even today I can remember every detail.
I was twelve when the American soldiers
came to our village . . .

79

The Identification

So you think its Stephen?
Then I'd best make sure
Be on the safe side as it were.
Ah, theres been a mistake. The hair
you see, its black, now Stephens fair . . .
Whats that? The explosion?
Of course, burnt black. Silly of me.
I should have known. Then lets get on.

The face, is that a face I ask?
that mask of charred wood
blistered, scarred could
that have been a child's face?
The sweater, where intact, looks
in fact all too familiar.
But one must be sure.

The scoutbelt. Yes thats his.
I recognise the studs he hammered in
not a week ago. At the age
when boys get clothes-conscious
now you know. Its almost
certainly Stephen. But one must
be sure. Remove all trace of doubt.
Pull out every splinter of hope.

Pockets. Empty the pockets.
Handkerchief? Could be any schoolboy's.
Dirty enough. Cigarettes?
Oh this can't be Stephen.
I dont allow him to smoke you see.
He wouldn't disobey me. Not his father.
But thats his penknife. Thats his alright.
And thats his key on the keyring
Gran gave him just the other night.
Then this must be him.

I think I know what happened
. . . . . . about the cigarettes
No doubt he was minding them
for one of the older boys.
Yes thats it.
Thats him.
Thats our Stephen.

ROGER McGOUGH

80

Kill the Children

On Hallowe'en in Ship Street,
quite close to Benny's bar,
the children lit a bonfire
and the adults parked a car.

Sick minds sing sentimental songs
and speak in dreary prose
and make ingenious home-made bombs –
and this was one of those.

Some say it was the UVF
and some the IRA
blew up that pub on principle
and killed the kids at play.

They didn't mean the children,
it only was the blast;
we call it KILL THE CHILDREN DAY
in bitter old Belfast.

JAMES SIMMONS

UVF: Ulster Volunteer Force
 IRA: Irish Republican Army

(These are two of the groups in Northern
Ireland who have committed themselves to
the use of violence for political ends.)

The Day of The Bomb

What might these people say?

a   A neighbour

b   A fireman

c   A mother of an injured child

d   The person who planted the bomb

e   A drinker in the pub

f   A father who had to identify his son

First Blood

It was. The breech smelling of oil,
The stock of resin—buried snug
In the shoulder. Not too much recoil
At the firing of the first slug.

(Jubilantly into the air)
Nor yet too little. Targets pinned
Against a tree: shot down: and there
Abandoned to the sniping wind.

My turn first to carry the gun.
Indian file and camouflaged
With contours of green shade and sun
We ghosted between larch and larch.

A movement between branches—thump
Of a fallen cone. The barrel
Jumps, making branches jump
Higher, dislodging the squirrel

To the next tree. Your turn, my turn.
The silhouette retracts its head.
A hit. 'Let's go back to the lawn.'
'We can't leave it carrying lead

'For the rest of its life. Reload.
Finish him off. Reload again.'
It was now *him*, and when he showed
The sky cracked like a window pane.

He broke away: traversed a full
Half dozen trees: vanished. Had found
A hole? We watched that terrible
Slow spiral to the clubbing ground.

His back was to the tree. His eyes
Were gun barrels. He was dumb,
And we could not see past the size
Of his hands or hear for the drum

In his side. Four shots point-blank
To dull his eyes, a fifth to stop
The shiver in his clotted flank.
A fling of earth. As we stood up

The larches closed their ranks. And when
Earth would not muffle the drumming blood
We, like dishonoured soldiers, ran
The gauntlet of a darkening wood.

JON STALLWORTHY

a   What is happening in the first two verses of the poem?

b   What signs make the two young hunters aware of the squirrel?

c   What phrase in the fifth verse describes the squirrel?

d   What is meant in verse 6 by: '*It* was now *him*'?

e   Try to describe the way that the boys feel as the squirrel falls and then lies on the ground.

f   Why do they fire so many shots into the squirrel?

g   After they have buried the squirrel, why do you think they run from the woods?

h   Choose two expressions that convey the horror of the killing for you. Say why you have chosen them.

Write about a time when you were involved in some activity that you realised was wrong. What did you do? How did you feel?

Plug In, Turn On, Look Out

Run for your lives, take to the hills,
The machines are on the march:
This morning my electric razor launched
A vicious and unwarranted attack on me—
It came at me, snarling through its
Thirty-four rotary teeth and
Flicking its flexy tail
(Fortunately I fought it off
With my dad's old cut-throat).
Do not turn your back on toasters,
The machines are taking over:
The talking weighing machines at Waterloo
Told me today in no uncertain terms,
Where I could stick my threepence—
I was trapped in the lift doors twice today,
Don't tell me it's coincidence;
So steer clear of vacuum cleaners, it's
The Mechanical Revolution:
I turned the telly on tonight and it
Turned itself off again . . .
If necessary, we must resort to
Underhand tactics—
Keep your electric lawnmower securely tethered,
Cut down supplies of food to your refrigerator,
Kick your car at regular intervals
(That's why the Lord gave you legs).
And above all, don't let them find out
Who's winning . . .

Meanwhile, I intend to lead
A picked band of desperadoes
In a death-or-glory attack
On the I.C.T. Computer Installation
(We must destroy
The brains behind this uprising).

PETER ROCHE

Of course, it isn't only machines that have their eyes on you.

Those harmless little pot plants that nice grannies have on every available shelf are just waiting for their opportunity.

As for the trees in the back garden, they're only waiting for the order from their leaders.

And what about the grass? One day you could be lying out in the sunshine when you feel the tiny blades begin to pierce your skin.

See if you can write your own piece in which plants take revenge for all these years of persecution by humans.

(And, whatever you do, don't let the cactus see what you are doing; it only gives her ideas.)

Requirements in the Shelter

'Clothing
Cooking Equipment
Food
Furniture
Hygiene
Lighting
Medical
Shrouds'

What?

'Shrouds.
Several large, strong, black plastic bags and a reel of 2-inch, or wider, adhesive tape
can make adequate air-tight containers for deceased persons until the situation
permits burial.'

No I will not put my lovely wife into a large strong black plastic bag
No I will not put my lovely children into large strong plastic bags
No I will not put my lovely dog or my lovely cats into large strong black
    plastic bags

I will embrace them all until I am filled with their radiation

Then I will carry them, one by one,
Through the black landscape
And lay them gently at the concrete door
Of the concrete block
Where the colonels
And the chief detectives
And the MPs
And the Regional Commissioners
Are biding their time

And then I will lie down with my wife and children and my dog and my
    cats

and we will wait for the door to open

ADRIAN MITCHELL

Adrian Mitchell's poem is based on official government advice in case of war.

If we are expected to listen to their advice, it seems only right and fair that they should
be willing to listen in turn.

What advice would you like to offer to the government?

(Try setting this out as a formal document with a series of points or as a formal letter.)

The Appeal

Don't give them your money.
They don't really need it.
It'll only create problems.
We need helpless people
and money wipes them out.
Too much food
and they'll have to
bring in the slimming pills.
Too much success
and they'll have to
fly in psychiatrists.
These folk have found the simple life,
the open-air life, the life
unencumbered by possessions,
by status.
Don't export the
curse of affluence
to the Third World.
They'll only become like us
or, if we give too freely,
we'll become like them.

STEVE TURNER

The Diet

Sat in the pub
Drink flowing free
Everyone's merry
Cept poor old me
I'm starving

I have to sit
in the corner
All quiet
The trouble you see
I'm on a diet
I'm starving

No whisky, no gin
Why did I come in
no ploughman's lunch
like that greedy bunch
I'm starving

Shall I walk to the bar
I won't go too far
Just a pkt of crisps
and one drink
I'm starving

Then I think I'll have
when I've finished this fag
some chicken and chips
in a basket
I'm starving

No I can't keep quiet
I'll shout, Bugger the diet
I'm absolutely starving

MAUREEN BURGE

Eat, Drink and Be Sick

Well, Happy Christmas, Father,
Have I got a treat for you!
A pair of socks in bottle green
And one in navy blue.
I wrapped them round your after-shave
And put them by the tree
And wrote me name in biro
So you'd know they came from me.

Well yes, I'll have a mince pie please
And then I'll have a date
And then I'll crack a nut or two
And fling them in the grate,
And then I'll have a fig
And then perhaps a glass of wine
And then another two or three
To make me forehead shine.

One cold turkey sandwich
But a *small* one, understand.
Look, the meat's all falling out –
You got a rubber band?
Stoke the fire up, Father,
Ram the poker down the back,
Those potatoes in the ashes
Well, they've never looked so black!

Well yes, I'll have a liqueur chocolate
With the crunchy sugar coat
That rattles round your teeth
And turns to gravel in your throat.
How nice the room looks, Mother,
With the tinsel round the walls,
I'll have an Advocaat then please,
Yes, that one there, the Bols.

Just one slice of Christmas cake
Then I shall have to run.
A tangerine then, if you *must* –
Just hold this Chelsea bun.
One glass of cherry brandy
No more crystal fruits for me!
Happy Christmas all!
I'm going home to have me tea!

PAM AYRES

The Hayes, Cardiff

for Robert Oats

Do you remember the beggar
we always saw,
perched high on the graveyard wall,
his body spreadeagled against wet
railings, as if crucified?

His mate with the knotted walking stick
collecting scraps into a paper bag
cursing the weather, and the children
shuffling about his feet
like frightened cats.

And like the Salvation Army
they were there each winter,
churning Christmas music from an
ageless accordion;

and we, like they, were never in a hurry,
sitting, talking, by the cockle stall
in the market entrance
and getting nowhere,
like the snow on the silver birches
sparkling in the sunshine.

GERAINT JARMAN

a   At what time of the year does this poem take place?

b   Why do you think the beggars play the accordion?

c   Why do you think that they choose this particular time of year?

d   Explain the difference between 'shuffling' and walking.

e   Say, in your own words, how the beggar stood on the graveyard wall.

f   What appears to be the children's attitude to the beggar's mate in the second verse?

g   What are the links between the beggars and the Salvation Army?

h   In what ways are the writer and his friend like the beggar and his mate?

Not Another Christmas

Bethlehem has not got much to recommend it. It is a small town with very little character and is crowded with narrow, dirty streets. Even today, many visitors are disappointed by the welcome they receive.

We can only guess what the welcome was like 2,000 years ago but this is how Harri Webb pictures it. Whenever I read this I always imagine the innkeeper's wife is speaking.

Never Again

You never saw such a stupid mess,
The government, of course, were to blame.
That poor young kid in her shabby dress
And the old chap with her, it seemed such a shame.

She had the baby in a backyard shed,
It wasn't very nice, but the best we could do.
Just fancy, a manger for a bed,
I ask you, what's the world coming to?

We're sorry they had to have it so rough,
But we had our troubles, too, remember,
As if all the crowds were not enough
The weather was upside-down for December.

There was singing everywhere, lights in the sky
And those drunken shepherds neglecting their sheep
And three weird foreigners in full cry—
You just couldn't get a good night's sleep.

Well now they've gone, we can all settle down,
There's room at the inn and the streets are so still
And we're back to normal in our own little town
That nobody's heard of, or ever will.

And though the world's full of people like those,
I think of them sometimes, especially her,
And one can't help wondering . . . though I don't suppose
Anyone will ever know who they were.

HARRI WEBB

Of course, any account will be biased. If she were really all that 'sorry', why didn't she find some space for the pregnant woman? Then there's the shepherds. She might have thought that they were drunk but I guess they'd explain it by saying that they were excited or overwhelmed.

After all, it's a rotten job looking after someone else's smelly sheep on freezing cold nights. How often do such people get visited by angels? And it must have been a bit unusual for them to risk their jobs by leaving their sheep alone on the hillside.

Imagine that you were one of the shepherds on that first Christmas. How would you tell the story?

Adrian Henri's Talking After Christmas Blues

Well I woke up this mornin' it was Christmas Day
And the birds were singing the night away
I saw my stocking lying on the chair
Looked right to the bottom but you weren't there
there was
        apples
           oranges
                chocolates
                    . . . aftershave
– but no you.

So I went downstairs and the dinner was fine
There was pudding and turkey and lots of wine
And I pulled those crackers with a laughing face
Till I saw there was no one in your place
there was
        mince pies
           brandy
                nuts and raisins
                    . . . mashed potato
– but no you.

Now it's New Year and it's Auld Lang Syne
And it's 12 o'clock and I'm feeling fine
Should Auld Acquaintance be Forgot?
I don't know girl, but it hurts a lot
there was
        whisky
           vodka
                dry Martini (stirred
                    but not shaken)
. . . and 12 New Year resolutions
– all of them about you.

So it's all the best for the year ahead
As I stagger upstairs and into bed
Then I looked at the pillow by my side
. . . I tell you baby I almost cried
there'll be
        Autumn
           Summer
                Spring
                    . . . and Winter
– all of them without you.

ADRIAN HENRI

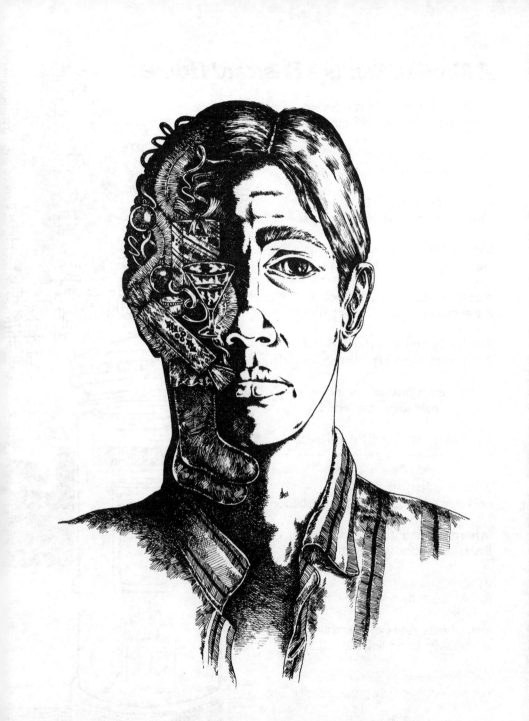

Christmas is fine if you have plenty of friends and the family get on together. As Adrian Henri remembers, it can be a pretty miserable time as well.

See if you can think of some of the situations which could spoil the Christmas celebrations.

Choose one of these situations and write your own Christmas story.

A Martian Sends a Postcard Home

Caxtons are mechanical birds with many wings
and some are treasured for their markings—

they cause the eyes to melt
or the body to shriek without pain.

I have never seen one fly, but
sometimes they perch on the hand.

Mist is when the sky is tired of flight
and rests its soft machine on ground:

then the world is dim and bookish
like engravings under tissue paper.

Rain is when the earth is television.
It has the property of making colours darker.

Model T is a room with the lock inside—
a key is turned to free the world

for movement, so quick there is a film
to watch for anything missed.

But time is tied to the wrist
or kept in a box, ticking with impatience.

In homes, a haunted apparatus sleeps,
that snores when you pick it up.

If the ghost cries, they carry it
to their lips and soothe it to sleep

with sounds. And yet, they wake it up
deliberately, by tickling with a finger.

Only the young are allowed to suffer
openly. Adults go to a punishment room

with water but nothing to eat.
They lock the door and suffer the noises

alone. No one is exempt
and everyone's pain has a different smell.

At night, when all the colours die,
they hide in pairs

and read about themselves—
in colour, with their eyelids shut.

CRAIG RAINE

Of course that Martian hasn't quite understood what happens on earth. Did you work out that what he calls 'caxtons' are, in fact, books? What are the 'many wings' that the Martians think books have?

See how much of the Martian's postcard you can explain.

What do you reckon a Martian would make of what goes on in a school?

- What would he call a school?
- What might he think it was?
- How would he explain classrooms?
- What would he make of the games lessons?
- What about teachers?
- And school meals?

Write home on behalf of our Martian including details of the school visit.

It helps to think first about who is writing to whom.

Is Martian cosmonaut Blutzi Schree writing to her husband Frunk who has been left at home to wash the nappies and look after their two little Martian sprogs?

Perhaps astro-engineer Gunkel Splatt is dropping a line to his girlfriend Greenee who works on the hover buses in Trinquilasee.

Alternatively Srosh Viday on his first trip as a space student could be writing back to his elderly Uncle Dirkwen who has just taken early retirement at 135. (Martians, of course, are usually in full-time employment between the ages of 30 and 150 years.)

Once you've got details like that sorted out, it ought to be a lot easier. For example . . .

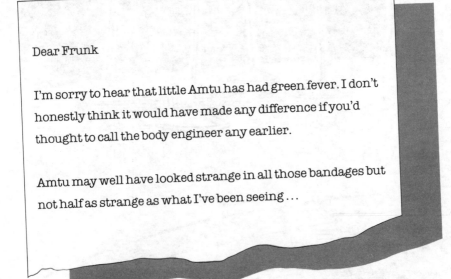

Dear Frunk

I'm sorry to hear that little Amtu has had green fever. I don't honestly think it would have made any difference if you'd thought to call the body engineer any earlier.

Amtu may well have looked strange in all those bandages but not half as strange as what I've been seeing . . .

After We've Gone

Who will live in our house
After we've gone
Will they have green plastic
Instead of a lawn?

Who will live in our house
After the wars?
Will there be mutations
That crawl on all fours?

Will the shiny robot workers
Be dreaming strange, new dreams?
Will the pigeons, big as turkeys
Roost on our ancient beams?

Who will use our kitchen?
What will they cook?
Who will sleep in our room
And how will they look?

Will they feel our ghosts disturbing
Their cybernetic years
With the echoes of our laughter
And the shadows of our tears?

Will there still be lovers?
Who will sing our songs?
Who will live in our house
After we've gone?

FRAN LANDESMAN

Technical Words

If you repair motor bikes you have to know, for example, what a friction disc anchor bolt is and what a sprocket locking plate does.

In the same way there are technical words that are used about poetry which it helps if you understand.

Alliteration   This happens where two or more closely connected consonants begin with the same sound.
e.g.   Anthony Thwaite in 'Hedgehog' (on page 57) calls the animal 'a country creature'.

Colloquial   If a poem sounds as if it has been written down just as an ordinary person would say something, then it is in colloquial language.
e.g.   Roger McGough's 'Nooligan' (on page 76) is written as if the hooligan is speaking directly to you in his own voice.

Image   A picture created by the words that a poet uses.
e.g.   Tony Connor's poem 'In Oak Terrace' (on page 26) leaves its readers with an image of an old and lonely woman.
Metaphors and similes are two examples of the way images are created. When you come across a question such as 'What imagery does the poet employ . . . ?' it is normally the use of simile and metaphor that the questioner has in mind.

Irony   A writer is adopting an ironic tone when he says one thing but it is clear that he means something very different, perhaps the exact opposite.
e.g.   Steve Turner's 'The Appeal' (on page 88).

Metaphor   One type of image. Instead of saying something is like something else, it is described as if it were literally that thing.
e.g.   In Phoebe Hesketh's poem 'Geriatric Ward' (on page 28) the doctor talks about how they 'spray cabbages with oxygen'. To the doctor, the old people have become cabbages, in his mind at least.

Metre   The rhythm of the lines in a poem based on the number and the pattern of stressed and unstressed syllables.
Metre doesn't make much sense until someone sits down and explains it to you. So if you are in the dark, ask.
A good example to get explained to you is 'Friends' (on page 11).

Narrative Verse   Poetry that tells a story.
e.g.   'The Gresford Disaster' (on page 33).

Narrator   The storyteller.
Quite often the character who is speaking in a poem is not the writer but someone the writer has met or has imagined.
e.g.   In 'A Girl's Song' by Leslie Norris (on page 56), the poet is putting words into the mouth of a woman who has loved and lost a sailor.

Rhyme

When two words both end with a similar sound they rhyme with each other – for example, 'more' and 'floor'. In poetry, the words that rhyme are usually to be found at the end of a line. In some poetry, the pattern of the rhymes is the same in each verse. You can see how this works by turning to 'The Gresford Disaster' (on page 33) or to 'Friends' (on page 11).

Simile

A comparison in which one thing is said to be similar to another.
e.g. In D. H. Lawrence's 'Beautiful Old Age' (on page 26) he says that old people are 'like apples' and 'like yellowing leaves'. While the word 'like' is most often found in a simile, the word 'as' is also used.
e.g. In 'Peerless Jim Driscoll' by Vernon Scannell (on page 4) the boxer is said to have a punch which is 'as clean as silver'.

Stanza

Another word meaning a verse of a poem.

Style

Not what you do but the way that you do it. Looking at a poet's style might mean looking at the words chosen, the kinds of pictures that are painted by the words, the use of rhythm, the lengths of sentences, and so on.

Symbol

A symbol is used to represent a group, an idea, or an object.
e.g. The cross is a symbol of Christianity and the heart on a Valentine card is a symbol of love.

Theme

The subject (or subjects) covered by a poem, not simply the facts but the ideas and thinking behind those facts.
e.g. One of the themes of 'Daily London Recipe' by Steve Turner (on page 36) is overcrowding in cities.

Tone

The mood of the poem. This is best understood by asking yourself what tone of voice would you use if you had to read the poem aloud.
e.g. The tone of Siegfried Sassoon's poem 'Atrocities' (on page 77) is angry and bitter. The poet clearly feels nothing but scorn for the ex-soldier who now spends his time drinking and telling lies about his time in the army. On the other hand, the tone in 'The Hayes, Cardiff' by Geraint Jarman (on page 91) is reflective, almost nostalgic.

Index of Authors